VICTIMPROOF

The Student's Guide to End Bullying

TOM THELEN

CHARACTER
PROGRAMS

CharacterPrograms.Org – *Resources for Life*

Published in Grand Rapids, Michigan, by Character Programs.

ISBN-13: 978-1499613711

ISBN-10: 1499613717

Illustrations by Simeon Cochrane. Used by Permission.

Font Design by Guillaume Séguin of Segments Design. Used by Permission.

Edited by Laura Wirick, Cindy Thelen, and Casie Thelen.

Accompanying DVD Curriculum Copyright © 2013 by Tom Thelen.

Videography by Dave Van Keulen, Jordan Niemeier, Joel Udell,
Cameron Versluis, Chandler Versluis, and Alexander Fayroyce Rozell.

To every student who feels victimized: hang in there.

You can't control whether or not you get bullied, but you *can* control whether or not you become a victim.

- Tom Thelen

Table of Contents

MODULE A   The # 1 Way To Stop Bullying

                 Introduction   i

Chapter 1   Victimproof   1

Chapter 2   Bullyproof   15

Chapter 3   Be The Change   33

MODULE B   **Ending Bullying From The Inside Out**

Chapter 4   Character   45

Chapter 5   Self-Esteem   57

Chapter 6   Self-Discipline   67

MODULE C   **Ending Bullying From The Outside In**

Chapter 7   Honesty   79

Chapter 8   Respect   89

Chapter 9   Responsibility   97

MODULE D   **Leading The Anti-Bullying Revolution**

Chapter 10   Purpose   107

Chapter 11   Teamwork   117

Chapter 12   Leadership   131

BONUS   Secrets to Success   143

    ○   Victimproof Pledge   147

    ○   Endnotes   149

    ○   About the Author   154

MODULE A

The #1 Way to Stop Bullying

introduction

Greetings Young Humanoid. It is I, Tom Thelen, author of this book, and wearer of huge glasses. I wrote Victimproof specifically for **you** because, well, I was you. As a teen I seemed like a normal kid on the outside, and I did what most kids do on the inside – I shoved my pain deep down so no one would think I was a freak. But since I was a bit of a freak, I still got bullied. I didn't know how to handle my pain, so I fought back to my bullies with sarcasm. I was the class clown. And over time, the kid who was bullied started to become a bully. Thankfully one teacher intervened in my life and everything changed.

The cool thing is that I was able to take the pain of my past and turn it into something beautiful. Today, my full-time job is speaking to students about bullying. Yes, I am a motivational speaker, and I live in a van down by the river. Well sort of. I actually live in a cute little neighborhood with my wife and our four kids (count 'em - four kids). So when I'm not out speaking to students I'm at home reminding Addie and Jack (the older two) to flush the toilet and reminding our twins Ellie and Lucy (the younger two) to go in the toilet. My wife Casie and I have been married since 2003 and she owns a small hair salon in our town.

As I meet students at schools and youth conferences, I keep being reminded of a few simple facts. First, tons of teens feel victimized by the problems they face in life – like they have no power to change their current circumstances. Second, many students feel alone in their struggles – like they're the only ones going through it. And third, most of them don't have a guide – someone to help lead them through the thick jungle of life.

So to the first group, I say… You have the power to change your life. You really do, and I promise to show an effective method to lose the victim mentality.

To the second, I say… You are not alone. I've been there, and I know that most of your peers are "there" right now too, even though they're acting like they've got it all together.

And to the third group, I say… This book will help guide you through the jungle of life but only as much as you take action and learn to help yourself.

You will notice that I teach from personal stories that happened to me as a teen, but I hope you also see that I'm teaching the same universal values that have been taught for centuries in every culture of the world. Iconic leaders from Jesus to Gandhi, to Martin Luther King Jr. have taught these principles and lived them out as examples for the rest of us, guiding us to true north.

So if you want to find your true north, use this book as more of a compass than a map.[1] Maps show you the exact route from here to there. Maps are great when you know exactly where you are and where you want to go. But in life, we all start in different places, and we want to end up in different places. Each of us has a unique journey to success. The compass is great because it always points north no matter what. Come rain or shine, the compass is always there to guide you. So let these principles guide you to true north.

You may recognize some of the book's material from the first edition of the book, originally titled Teen Leadership Revolution. This updated version is packed with brand new content, loaded with over 30 new videos, and tightened up to focus on bullying and freeing students from the victim mindset.

Last thing: I'm going against the advice of my peers by releasing the first module of this book and the video curriculum FOR FREE. Yep, free download, no gimmicks. And the only thing I ask of you in return is this: *if the book speaks to you, if it helps you in some real way, then share it with another teen or teacher in your life.* You have my permission: post away on Facebook, Twitter, Google, etc. Pay it forward.

So buckle up.

You're about to become VICTIMPROOF.

1. V⚡CTIMPROOF

Sometimes I wish there was a way to re-write this story with me playing the part of the hero. But the truth is, I was a victim, and I felt completely powerless to change it.

At least that's how this all started.

In early high school I felt like a loser. And let me tell you, when you feel like a loser, you walk around with your head hung low. That's how it starts when you're becoming a victim. I should know – I was one.

Victims are always at the mercy of life circumstances. It's everyone else's fault. They have no control over it. They play the blame game saying things like: *I had no choice! You made me do this! Why do I always get singled out? No one else has to do it. It's not fair! Everyone's out to get me!*

Seriously, it's like walking around with a big sign on your back that says **"Bully me! I'm an easy target!"**

And that was me. Leading up to my sophomore year in high school, I had developed a victim mentality. Life had dealt me a bad hand. I was short for my age, I had allergies and asthma, my dad hated me (I thought), my teachers wanted me to fail, and on and on. The truth was, there were a lot of things I didn't like about myself. And since there were so many things I didn't like about myself, I decided to do the most logical thing and just... be somebody else.

So I became Funny Tom. I was like, *"WhaHoo! Look at me everyone! (...insert funny joke here...)"*. Funny Tom made everyone laugh, which felt really good. Funny Tom was the life of the party, which felt really important. Pushing the envelope of acceptable behavior was my new drug of choice. It was addicting. I would do anything to get a laugh: make fun of myself, make fun of my friends, my teachers, you name it.

My life was on a slippery slope, but at the time I didn't even know it. At the age of 15, I wasn't thinking about slippery slopes. I had my class-clown image to maintain. That was my new fulltime job. But the tough part about trying so hard to be someone else is that it becomes very difficult to be... yourself.

Because you're busy being someone else!

Who cares! I was busy being Funny Tom, and it felt good, dag nabbit.

But not everyone was laughing. In my acting out, I was starting to miss assignments at school. I was mouthing off to all the wrong people at all the wrong times. At home, the conflict between my parents and I was getting worse every day, and they were threatening to kick me out of the house. Verbal fights with my dad were starting to turn into physical fights with my dad.

Abuse was becoming normal.

And yet I covered it up every day with a class clown smile. It was obvious to everyone except me: the wheels of my life were starting to fall off.

Then I was called to a "special meeting" at my school. The meeting itself didn't make me feel very special at all, but what followed the meeting would change my life forever.

THE INTERVENTION

So there I was, sitting in the classroom with all my teachers, the principal, my parents, and me.

Just me.

Surrounded by people, but completely alone.

I wanted to melt through the floor, or better yet, strap on some jet pack and shoot out the window, saluting the crowd with my middle finger. *Take that, suckers!*

None of that happened. Instead, I was put on academic probation, which is a fancy way of saying *"One more thing, and you're out of here Mister!"*

After the meeting, my English Teacher, Mrs. Burdick, asked if she could talk with me and my parents. She told us about a counseling program that she and Mr. Burdick offered on their farm. It was a three-week program for young men who needed a "character intervention," whatever that meant. The Burdicks had been in education and farming for many years, and now as young grandparents, they offered a counseling program for teens ages 12 to 15.

Mrs. Burdick said it was too-late for many boys my age since the "concrete of life was already setting up." But then she said something I never forgot. She said she still believed there was hope for me. She still believed I could change – if I wanted to. And right then and there she asked if I wanted to come to the counseling program.

Three weeks.　　On a farm.　　In counseling.

My head was spinning. I was thinking,

I don't wanna go! All my friends will find out. Everyone will know that I'm a failure. I'll never get a girlfriend. No one will like me. They'll think I'm a freak! THERE IS NO WAY I'M GOING TO DO THIS!

But through my tears and insecurities, I heard my own voice say, "Yeah, I'll go." And then I said to myself, *"Shut up Voice! Who asked you anyway?!!"*

I really came that close to saying no. I mean I almost gave in to my fears and insecurities. Then I realized something: Mrs. Burdick was *for me,* not against me. She wanted me to succeed, and she was willing to invest in me. She believed in me even when I didn't believe in myself. The whole time my brain was shouting at me, telling me not to go, but my heart was saying something different.

My heart said go.

Sometimes the hardest decisions in life can also be the best decisions you ever make.

So I went.

Life on the Burdick Farm was tough. I had to wake up each morning at 5 AM to do the farm chores before school. Then, even after a full day of school, I was in charge of making supper every night. And I was a terrible cook (still am to this day, thank you very much).

Very tolerant people, the Burdicks, or maybe they just had low standards for food. My meals were pretty nasty, but they didn't complain.

And after supper they would counsel me. I remember them saying **"Tom, you are not a victim**... you always have the ability to respond... and your response is your responsibility."

They taught me about the *fight or flight* instinct – that our natural response to conflict is to fight back or to run away. I realized I had been fighting back to my bullies and to my dad. Not with my fists, but with my words.

bitterness

They told me that underneath that class clown image, they saw a very hurt student – a student weighed down by bitterness. And I remember thinking, *"Bitterness? What are they even talking about? I never chose to become bitter!"*

But guess what I learned along the way? Bitterness is not something you choose. Bitterness chooses you.

Bitterness settles into your life like dust settles on the TV screen. It's like, *How did that dust even get there?* It got there because it exists in a world with dust. Simple as that. And if you exist in a world with unresolved conflicts, hidden hurts, and secrets, you're going to develop some bitterness.

It's that pain that eats at your soul reminding you of who hurt you, begging you to try and settle the score.

It's like renting out free space in your head to the person who hurt you. You think about them all the time as you play out revenge fantasies to the silent movie in your mind.

It's like a poisonous seed that grows up into your life and suffocates your heart until you're only a shell of the person you used to be. It starts killing you from the inside out.

And here's the nasty part: as those dark thoughts swirl around in your head, you become the prisoner! You end up doing the time for someone else's crime. You get taken hostage by the pain. It is absolutely crazy – the best parts of your soul are consumed by resentment, and yet the score remains unsettled.

And that is the subtle lie of bitterness: that we should repay an eye for an eye, a tooth for a tooth, and that in doing so, the score will finally be even.

The problem is that "even" never comes, and revenge only escalates the problem.

FORGIVE

The principle of forgiveness has been taught all throughout history. The famous peace advocate Mahatma Gandhi used to say *"An eye for an eye only makes the whole world blind."* [2] In other words, repaying evil with evil only creates more evil. Jesus taught his followers to forgive people *"not seven times, but seventy times seven."* [3] And throughout the ages, the greatest leaders have called us back to this ancient principle.

I remember the Burdicks asking me if I could forgive my bullies and if I could forgive my dad.

I was thinking, *"Why on earth would I want to do that? Why would I let them off the hook for what they did to me?"*

But in that moment I was missing the point. For real, check this out: if you get nothing else out of this book, get this… Forgiveness is not about letting someone else off the hook for what they did to you. No. Forgiveness is about letting yourself off the hook for having to carry that pain into your future life.

So I began to forgive my bullies. I began to forgive my dad. I even started forgiving myself for the things I didn't like about me. And let me tell you: it has made all the difference.

○ ○ ○

and Forget?...

One of the most popular sayings about forgiveness is "Forgive and forget." People tell you to move on and act like it never happened. "Get over it." But could there be some kind of unhealthy denial in forgetting what happened to you? I mean, if you forgive and forget are you supposed to go back to the same abusive environment? Are you supposed to become a doormat, so people can walk all over you the rest of your life?

No flippin way.

For me, one of the most powerful parts of forgiveness has been "re-releasing" the desire for revenge whenever the memories come back. I don't go out of my way to remember it; traumatic events have a way of coming back on their own even when you've already forgiven someone. A familiar voice or a certain smell takes you right back. You drive by the house where "it" happened, and suddenly you're transported back in time. And in that moment, the temptation is to relive the pain and hold on to the resentment.

Resist! The memories will come back whether you want them to or not, sometimes years after the initial offense, sometimes through something completely unrelated. So when they do come, you have to be ready to **remember what you learned from it, and then re-release the desire for revenge.** In that moment, remember how that person taught you what *not* to do. Think about how you can avoid spreading that same type of hurt into someone else's life. Remember that setting up healthy boundaries with abusive people helps keep your heart alive. Think about how forgiveness allows you to trust again – how it helps you establish authentic relationships with healthy people.

Remembering can actually propel you forward, so you can turn the pain of your past into something beautiful. Maybe the greatest purpose of your life is actually through the fire of your pain. Maybe because you went through "it" way back when, you can become the best person to help others through it in the future.

So don't try to forget it. Learn from it.

How many adults in your life are still being held back by their past? Seriously, if you can get this principle of forgiveness now while you're young, you will be emotionally ahead of many adults in your life. You will set yourself free to become the best version of yourself, and you will turn your pain into a purpose.

My dad and I actually have a great relationship today (crazy, right?). It's because my parents got help too. After my time on the farm, they ended up going to monthly counseling sessions for the next three years where they worked through their stuff. And I'm very, VERY grateful.

Today my fulltime job is speaking to students, and sometimes when I travel I get a voicemail from my dad saying something like this:

> *"Tom, I prayed for you this morning. I want you to know that I am so proud of you. I'm proud that you're taking the pain of our family's past and turning it into something beautiful. Do great today. I know you will. Love you."*

Wow. Like I said, I have a lot to be thankful for.

But listen, you might not be that lucky. You might not have parents who learn this stuff and work through their junk. They may keep puking up their pain on you. So remember: you don't have to carry it.

It's not what happens to you. It's how you deal with it.

As a healthy person, it's your job to accept responsibility for your life, your actions, and your outcomes. So stay focused on what you can control.

You can't control your parents and you can't control whether or not you get bullied, but you **can** control whether or not you become a victim.

When you learn to forgive, drop the blame, and release the pain, that's when you truly become…

Victimproof.

CHAPTER 1 DISCUSSION GUIDE

1. Watch the video curriculum at **Victimproof.com**.

2. What part of this chapter stood out to you the most and why? What part of the videos spoke to you?

3. What does it look like when someone plays the blame game? What do you think motivates it?

4. Have you ever tried to "be somebody else" at your school? Why do you think so many teens have a hard time being themselves?

5. Do you think it's possible to be victimized by something but not remain a victim forever? Why?

6. Why is the principle of forgiveness easy to understand but hard to live out?

7. What do you think of the idea of forgiving and then remembering so you can learn from it?

8. CHALLENGE: Think of one person you need to forgive (for your sake), and then spend some time forgiving them and releasing the desire for revenge.

2. bullyproof

I gasped for breath as the bully pulled my head out of the water for a brief second, only to slam me back beneath the cold waves of Gull Lake. I was thirteen and at summer camp. I'll never forget that day. How many times does someone have to hold your head under water to completely break your willpower? I would say about six times. Yes, six times will do it. I remember choking out swear words at the bully in between submersions, but I eventually gave up. There was nothing I could do physically, verbally, or emotionally to stop him. I felt like such a loser. A small crowd gathered but no one stood up for me, and no one talked about it afterward.

Neither did I. I wanted that event erased from history.

Almost all of us have experienced moments like this where we were at the complete mercy of a bully. 90% of students between the 4th and 8th grade report being victims of bullying.[4] Nine out of ten students – that's pretty much all of us. And for many kids, the bullying starts at an early age.

I remember when it first hit home with our kids. We were taking them out to the Kiddie Casino (aka - Chuck E. Cheese). At the time, Addie was five, Jack was three, and our twins, Ellie and Lucy, were one. Toward the end of the night we told Addie she had five minutes left to play. She bounded off with freedom while Casie and I kept an eye on the younger three. The five minutes came and went, and we started to look for Addie. She was nowhere to be found. Panic started to set in, and we began to fear the worse. But just then I spotted her. She was up high inside the giant play structure... cornered and crying in a tunnel. I waved at her, telling her to come down. Eventually she arrived at the bottom of the slide, soaked in her own tears.

What's wrong honey? Are you okay?

I couldn't come down because of the bullies. (She said, sobbing into my shirt.)

What do you mean, honey? What happened?

The bullies wouldn't let me come down. They called

me stupid and said I was a little poop head, so I had to stay up there. Now I'm never gonna go back.

She went on to describe the whole story and how she hadn't provoked them and hadn't fought back – the only thing she could do was run to the other end of the tunnel. We explained how proud we were of her for not trying to hurt them back, but even with our encouragement she still cried most of the way home. Since then we've had some frank discussions about how to recognize and respond to bullying.

Calling someone a stupid poop-head might not seem like much to you, but put yourself in the shoes a five year old little girl. Two boys twice your size give you your first verbal beat down, just for the fun of it. Meanwhile you're all alone with no one to rescue you.

It was traumatizing. Addie met her first bullies.

Stories like these are more common than you might think, and for many students, it only gets worse as they get older.

Hi, my name is Bob

I recently spoke at a conference for the National Association of Student Councils, and after my first speech I met a student named Pat (I've changed his real name for the sake of privacy). Pat was a bright young guy, about 16, who had just been voted to the National Board of Directors for the conference. Quite an accomplishment for such a young teen. He explained to me how he had attended a private school for most of his life, but after years of relentless bullying and after a verbal lashing from a teacher (in front of his whole class), his parents let him drop out and switch to a public school. The new school was a chance to start over, so that's exactly what he did. But this time things would be different. He had been picked on and bullied his whole life for his name, but at the new school no one had to know his real name. So during the first six months he told everyone his name was Bob. Out of all the names he could have picked, he chose Bob. He didn't go with anything exotic, like Fabian, or Marc-Anthony. Nope… just Bob.

Pat was willing to give up his own identity to avoid the bullying and ridicule that had followed him since grade school. He was willing to become a completely different person. This was a reasonable choice to him.

When the truth eventually came out, he was devastated, and he found himself, once again, starting all over trying to win new friends.

○ ○ ○

How far are you willing to run from your bullies? To another room? To another school? Another life?

If you feel alone or depressed, it's time to get help… like right now. It's time to talk with a trusted adult. Harming the bully or harming yourself is never the solution. There really is a better way.

THE CURRENT SYSTEM

In the 1970s, a psychology professor named Dr. Dan Olweus began surveying schools to get accurate data on bullying.[5] Since that time, the subject has grown into a whole field of study with mountains of evidence for schools to sift through. Over the years, the research has done a great job of identifying the extent of the problem, but it has done a poor job of finding solutions that actually work to reduce bullying. In over 30 years of anti-bullying research and prevention programs, the problem of bullying still taunts us, and new studies show it is actually getting worse.[6] But why? Most bullying prevention programs assume the victimization of students, so they focus on teaching kids how to get help. Students are taught to anticipate being bullied and to report every incident. The message:

VICTIMS + HELP + BOUNDARIES = PREVENTION

The traditional goal is to end all bullying and create bully-free schools. This is a noble concept, so why hasn't it worked? Where are all the bully-free schools? We've had 30-plus years of research and 30-plus years of solutions. Where are the success stories?

Answer: There aren't any. They don't exist.

The truth is: the problem of bullying isn't going away… because people aren't going away. Dealing with difficult people is something you will have to face the rest of your life. Even if your teachers could create a 100% bully-free school, it would not prepare you to face the real world after high school where there is no virtual-police to swoop in and save you from the mean looks of your coworkers or to rescue you from the hurtful posts on Facebook and Twitter.

Despite their stated intentions, many anti-bullying programs end up creating a "victim-culture." When the only solution is "REPORT ALL BULLYING!" it subtly communicates that students are destined to be bullied, helpless to speak up, and 100% dependent on the system for help. Are we accidentally creating a system of helplessness? A culture of victims?

○ ○ ○

Please don't misunderstand. I am not suggesting we throw out the bullying prevention programs and leave students to fend for themselves. We need the programs and policies, but we can't stop there. We have to go deeper and speak to the hearts of the students themselves. If we really want to *prevent* bullying, we have to change our focus. We must learn how to turn **victims into victors.**

bullying basics

The U.S. Government recently launched a new website called StopBullying.Gov where they define bullying as *"unwanted, aggressive behavior among school aged children that involves a real or perceived **power imbalance**. The behavior is repeated, or has the potential to be repeated, over time."* [7] I want you to focus in on that power imbalance. That's what bullying is – it's a power grab.

We see this in the animal kingdom when the "alpha" (the biggest, most aggressive animal) assumes control over the herd, physically dominating the other animals to bring them under his control. But we are not animals. We live in a civil society where all people are created equal. Short and tall, black and white – we all have equal value.

So in schools, the bullying power-grab is usually grouped into these four categories:

1. PHYSICAL BULLYING: Hitting, pushing, spitting, violence, taking someone's things.

2. VERBAL BULLYING: Name calling, sexual harassment, teasing, taunting.

3. SOCIAL BULLYING: Excluding someone on purpose, publically embarrassing someone.

4. CYBERBULLYING: online harassment, sharing inappropriate photos, texts, or threats.

We've researched it, labeled it, and tried to solve it, yet the bullying still continues on every campus. More students than ever are crying "bully" even when there is no power imbalance. Friends who take a joke too far tell their parents they've been bullied. They go to the school, file the forms, and then what? The school sits both students down, and then both students end up feeling like victims.

We cannot escape the truth that the current system of bullying prevention is broken in most schools. So what can be done? How can we shake the victim-culture?

a new old way

Instead of asking, *"How can we eliminate bullying?,"* we need to start asking, *"How can we turn victims into victors? How can we develop healthy students who can withstand the storms of life and respond appropriately to bullying and conflict?"*

The answer is surprisingly simple, and yet incredibly profound. It's called: **The Golden Rule:** *"Do unto others as you would have them do unto you."* [8] In other words: treat everyone the way you want to be treated – especially your enemies. And as easy as this sounds, it is actually very difficult to apply because it goes against the animal instinct to defend and fight back. The beauty is: when you love your enemies **it empowers you, and it removes the power of the bullying.** They go out of control, and you stay in control.

This universal principle has been taught through the ages by iconic leaders from Confucius to Buddha to Jesus who said in Luke 6:27, *"Love your enemies, do good to those who hate you."* [9] In today's world of common sense, The Golden Rule gives us much needed uncommon sense.

Now, it is important to note that this principle was never intended merely for your friends. Everyone likes people who like them back. It was created as a principle for how to deal with difficult people: how to deal with bullies. The Golden Rule is an incredibly refreshing concept. Instead of learning to keep score, the new solution becomes:

LOVE + BOUNDARIES + HELP = VICTORS

Learning this strategy will empower you and literally change your future. You can respond to bullies without fighting back or running away! You can live life as a VICTIM or as a VICTOR – it's your choice.

3 Ways To Lose The Victim Mindset...

1: become VICTimPROOF

- **Forgive Your Bullies.** Forgive them not for their sake, but for your sanity. They may never ask for forgiveness, but that's not your problem. You deserve to live a life free from bitterness.

- **Laugh It Off.** Being able to laugh at your own quirks is a sign of being a healthy person, so don't take life too seriously. You can cry about everything and empower the bully, or you can laugh it off and empower yourself.

- **Talk It Through.** Holding your thoughts and feelings inside only makes you go crazy. You weren't meant to carry it alone, so find a good friend and a trusted adult and tell them what's going on.

2: become bullyPROOF

- **Set Boundaries With Bullies.** It's your job to tell a hurtful person when they've crossed the line. Most of the time bullies don't realize how much harm they're causing, so say something like this: "I don't like that. Please stop."

- **Turn Your Bully Into a Friend.** Why do bullies bully? Because they're hurting inside and they want to feel powerful. It's a simple fact of life that hurt people hurt people. So have an attitude of grace toward bullies. You might be the very friend they need.

- **Get Help From An Adult.** When the bullying is physical, sexual, or repeated, you need to get help from a trusted adult right away. It takes guts, but you have to tell a teacher or a parent what happened. SO GO GET HELP!

3: become cultureproof

- **Be The Change.** When you see something that needs to change, that's when you know you have to be the change. You have the power to speak up whenever you see bullying happen in person or online. And more than half of the time when you do, the bullying stops within 10 seconds.[10] It's hard to ignore the peer pressure and become the first fish to swim upstream, but you have to do it. Don't offer the silent support of a bystander – **be an upstander!**

- **Move Together Against Bullying.** Create an anti-bullying group to help set the social tone at your school. Create a culture of character, so bullying is viewed as abnormal. Remember: it takes a long time to change a school culture, and some people will even make fun of you in the process, but it's totally worth it. You could literally save someone's life.

Together, these solutions can create a new culture at your school, but they only work when you take action.

You may have been hurt by a bully in your past. You may have been victimized, but it's your choice to remain a victim or to become a victor.

○ ○ ○

Cyberbullying 101

One of the most common questions I get from students and parents is "How do you stop teens from cyberbullying?" Adults in particular have a hard time with this because they didn't grow up with IPad and smartphones. Back in the day, they could get away from their bullies by physically avoiding them. But today it's different. With Facebook, Twitter, and social media sites, bullies can actually follow you home right into your pocket. This is serious stuff. A recent poll showed that students who are cyberbullied are three times more likely to attempt suicide, compared to students who are not bullied.[11]

I compiled the following guidelines in a list I like to call The Ten Commandments of Cyberbullying. As you read through it, think about how each principle applies to your most recent conflict online.

The Ten Commandments of
CYBERBULLYING

1. Thou shalt honor thy profile and keep it clean.

2. Thou shalt not post private or personal information.

3. Thou shalt not post hurtful comments or images.

4. Thou shalt not steal thy neighbor's online identity.

5. Thou shalt speak up for thy neighbor when he or she is cyberbullied.

6. Thou shalt unfriend or block cyberbullies when they refuse to stop.

7. Thou shalt have important conversation in person, not on the web.

8. Thou shalt remember that web posts are forever.

9. Thou shalt print off hurtful posts or archive them with TruthLocker[12] (free smartphone app).

10. Thou shalt report cyberbullying to a trusted adult when it is serious, sexual, and when in doubt.

This list is a good starting point, but remember: *rules alone* cannot prevent cyberbullying. Even the best guidelines and education won't stop it. Everything still rises and falls on the knee-jerk responses of imperfect people like you and me, people who are often more bold online than in real life. So when we experience cyberbullying, we have to rely on our character to respond respectfully, keeping us victimproof on the inside and bullyproof on the outside.

○ ○ ○

One of the nasty side effects of bullying is that sometimes the bullied kid becomes the bully. By late middle school, this was the case for me. I was tired of being called short, being excluded from social groups, and generally being pushed around. I let the bullies get to me, and I became a very bitter person. Overtime, I found myself using sarcasm to lift myself up while putting other people down. I was being a bully, and I didn't even realize it. And without the intervention and love of one teacher, my life would have continued down that path.

As you read this, you might realize that - at times - you have been the bully. You and your friends have been the ones to cause the pain. You intentionally excluded someone from your group, or you made fun of someone for the way they looked. But today is a new day. Right now is the time to go and make things right.

So if you're brave enough, put the book down and go do the right thing. **Now** is the time to be the change.

For real. You won't regret it.

I promise you.

○ ○ ○

All students witness bullying. It will happen around you before you even realize it, and you will find yourself being a bystander. The important thing to remember is to decide ahead of time how you will respond. Will you just sit there in silence, providing an audience for the bully, becoming a silent supporter? Or will you face your fears, speak up for the silent, and help create a new culture at your school?

We must empower our bullying prevention programs with the wisdom of The Golden Rule to help change victims to victors and bystanders to upstanders. Working together, we can create a culture of character in our schools. This is our shared mission.

It truly is a new (old) way.

CHAPTER 2 DISCUSSION GUIDE

1. Watch the video curriculum at **Victimproof.com**.

2. When was the first (or last) time a bully got the best of you? How did you respond?

3. Is there a "victim culture" at your school? What can you do to change your school's culture?

4. How does The Golden Rule empower students and remove power from bullies?

5. Which of the three solutions do you need to work on the most and why? (Victimproof, Bullyproof, or Cultureproof?)

6. Think of the last time you or one of your friends were cyberbullied? How did you respond? Why?

7. List at least three specific ways you can help stop cyberbullying.

8. If you could convince your friends to do one thing about bullying at your school, what would it be?

3. Be the change

You never know when you will be called upon to be the change. Throughout life there will be moments that come where you will be the only person in a position to help out or to speak up for someone in need. This was my moment.

A few years ago I got a phone call from a guy named Albeno. Albeno had recently moved to our area of Michigan with his brother, his brother's wife, and their two kids. At the time, my wife and I owned a large rental home, and Albeno called asking about renting it out. So like any rental situation, I checked Albeno's references: I did a credit check, I did a background check, I called his references. Everything checked out, so we rented the home to Albeno and his family.

After they moved in, my wife and I realized they were one of the only minority families living in the town. Since they didn't know many people, we thought maybe we should befriend them. What if we could be the change? So we started to get to know them. We would stop by to visit, Casie would bake cookies and drop them off, and slowly we began to establish a relationship with their family. They were very hospitable, always welcoming our company.

At the time, we lived about a half-hour away from the rental home, and the problem was: we gradually began to fade out of their lives. Our visits became less frequent and my phone calls to Albeno became few and far between. Sometimes I would think in the back of my mind: *It's been over a month since you talked with Albeno. You were going to be the change.* I felt like I let myself down, but even worse, I let Albeno down.

There will always be a million reasons to not be the change. You're too busy, or they live too far away, or no one else is doing it. Too many reasons.

Then one day, out of the clear blue, I got a phone call from Albeno. At this point it had been a couple months since we last talked. He was in a panic.

He said, *"Tom it's Albeno. Do you know a lawyer who speaks Spanish?"*

I was taken back. I was like, *"Well, my older sister is a lawyer, but she doesn't speak Spanish. What's going on Albeno?!!"*

He said, *"Tom, you may not know it, but my brother and I actually have a third brother who's still in Mexico..."*

He went on to describe the situation. The third brother and his wife had a son named Ronaldo, Albeno's nephew. Little Ronaldo was four years old, but his health was so bad that he only weighed 18 pounds. He had a tracheotomy in his neck, and he needed machines to breathe for him.

About a month prior to our phone call, the doctors in Mexico had declared there was no more hope for Ronaldo, so they decided to pull the plug. To them, his life wasn't worth saving. But Albeno and his family weren't willing to let that happen, so they made plans for a woman from Texas to fly to Mexico and pick up Ronaldo. On the flight back his battery powered breathing equipment gave out and he almost died on the plane, but they revived him on the runway. Then a woman from Michigan went to Texas and flew with Ronaldo to Michigan. Again his medical equipment failed, and he nearly died.

Albeno told me that for the past month his nephew Ronaldo was being nursed back to health at the Children's Hospital in Grand Rapids Michigan. *"That sounds good."* I said, *"…So why do you need a lawyer?"*

He said:

> *Tom, today I found out they're going to take him away from us. Someone has decided that our home is not fit for raising a child, so today they're going to put him into foster care.*

You never know when you will be called upon to be the change. I swallowed hard because I realized what day it was. I said:

> *Albeno… you are not going to believe this, but my kids actually have some health issues of their own. And once a year my kids have an appointment at the Children's Hospital in Grand Rapids where they get blood drawn to check on their protein levels and their metabolic rates. Albeno, the day for that appointment is TODAY! We are getting in the car right now Albeno. We will be there in twenty minutes.*

We were going to the very hospital where he was at.

We got to the hospital and got the kids checked in. Soon, I left Casie with the kids and raced up to the sixth floor to meet Albeno. I walked into the room and tears came to my eyes. Looking over to the bed, I saw a little boy who was just a shell of the person he used to be. Skin and bones.

I said, *"Where's the social worker?"* And Albeno pointed to a lady near the nurse's desk. I walked out of the room ready to speak for the family. But before I could get my first sentence out, she cut me off and said, *"Nope. I'm sorry, but I can't talk with you. You aren't family. I'm not allowed to talk with you."*

My heart sank into the pit of my stomach. This was supposed to be my chance to be the change, and then it was ripped from my fingers. I asked Albeno what we could do, and he replied, *"I don't know Tom, but the decision is being made in one hour at the courthouse."*

"I'll be there." I said.

The hour passes and anxiety starts to race through my mind. *I don't know anything about the court or the law. What am I supposed to say? Do I have to object or something? Am I supposed to wear a suit? How does this work?*

We arrived and took the elevator to the 4th floor. It was an "arbitration meeting" where the facts of the case would be argued before bringing a recommendation to the judge. At the head of a huge conference table sat a woman with stacks of papers in front of her. She was the arbitrator. She was there to help guide the discussion and make sure everything was recorded. To her left was a lawyer and a Child Protective Services Worker, and they were saying things like:

"We don't know that this home is fit for raising a child. We have no evidence to prove that it is. Further, we don't know if Ronaldo's parents are ever coming up from Mexico, and as such, we will recommend to the judge today that Ronaldo is pulled from the home and placed into the foster care system."

Albeno and I were seated next to each other on the other side of the table. He had his hand raised in the air desperate for help.

"Just tell us what to do, and we'll do it! We want Ronaldo to stay with us."

"I'm sorry." they said. *"Does anyone else have something to say?*

I felt my hand go up.

I swallowed hard and said:

"I am not related to Albeno or Ronaldo, but I am Albeno's landlord. And when we agreed to rent to their family, we did a credit check, and it checked out. And we did a criminal background check, and it checked out. We called their references, and everything checked out. We found out that Albeno is a high school graduate, and that he is here legally. We learned that the family attends church every weekend – they're people of faith. My wife and I spent time getting to know them, and every time

we've visited the home they have always kept it meticulously clean. They are people of integrity, people of character. And what's more, this home that you speak of is huge. It's five bedrooms, three and a half bathrooms. It's so big, that when Ronaldo's parents do make it up to Michigan, there will be plenty of room for all of them to stay together. This home is fit for raising a child."

○ ○ ○

And you should have been there that day. You should have been there to see the look in the eyes of that lawyer and that CPS worker. The look in their eyes began to change. Their faces began to soften.

Why? Because love has the ability to overcome the deepest hate. Love can overcome the greatest racism, or the worst assumptions we have about people who don't look like us.

There is no greater power than love.

And as the conversation unfolded, the whole spirit of the room changed. The lady with all the papers wrapped things up and said

Okay, I believe we have consensus. We will now go before the judge, but we will make a new recommendation. We will recommend that Ronaldo gets to stay with his family.

That is the power you have to be the change in someone else's life.

Ronaldo has since then regained much of his health, and he's living with his family. His parents made it to the United States, and they are very proud of their son.

And so am I.

○ ○ ○

Gandhi, the religious leader and peace advocate, was famous for saying, *"Be the change you wish to see in the world."* I love that. Don't wait around for everyone else to do it. You be the change. When the moment comes, you be the one to rise up. Become a voice for the voiceless, help for the helpless.

It grates against my soul that only 10% of students are willing to speak up when they see bullying happen right in front of them.[13] This is true for school campuses across America. Schools just like yours. It's called being a bystander. And the crazy part is, it actually empowers the bully to have an audience, so bystanders – whether they know it or not – end up becoming silent supporters of the bully.

Students don't plan on being bystanders. The bullying just happens right in front of them on the school bus or in the lunch room. And most students just freeze up. They don't do anything.

This has to change. It must change.

It is the driving passion of my life to empower students to be the change on their campus, whatever that looks like. It might mean sitting with the unpopular kid on the wrong side of the cafeteria. It might mean wearing less name-brand clothes to start friendships with kids who have less money than you. It might mean speaking up when you see someone getting bullied.

There will be times in the next month, in the next week, maybe even in the next day, where you will be the only person in a position to be the change. And if you don't speak up, it won't happen.

When you see something that needs to change, that's when you know you must be the change.

CHAPTER 3 DISCUSSION GUIDE

1. Watch the video curriculum at **<u>Victimproof.com</u>**.

2. What part of this chapter stood out to you the most and why? What part of the videos spoke to you?

3. Why do you think only 10% of students speak up when they see bullying happen?

4. Where on your campus is bullying most likely to happen, and what can you do to help stop it?

5. List two or three historical leaders and discuss how they became the change.

6. Discuss some of the changes needed in your school's culture.

7. What are some challenges you could face in being the change?

8. CHALLENGE: Write down a commitment to being the change in one specific area.

MODULE B

Ending Bullying From The Inside-Out

4. CHARACTER

In early high school my character wasn't very strong. I endured school by doing as little work as possible and having as much fun as I could. The only thing I worked hard on was getting laughs and pulling off pranks.

One time my friends and I toilet papered a house with over 100 rolls of toilet paper. Now that was an expensive prank. At that point it feels like less of a prank and more of a financial investment. I was into toilet paper like bankers were into stocks and bonds.

I was missing a lot of assignments at school, and the ones I turned in were not my best work. Why worry about homework? My focus was on being the life of the party. I could get a whole crowd of students laughing, but usually at someone else's expense. The truth was: I was becoming a bully and I didn't even know it. Eventually my behavior started to catch up with me, and that's what landed me on the Burdick's farm.

Every night for three weeks Mr. and Mrs. Burdick would counsel me after dinner.

I will never forget them saying:

> *Tom, your character is pretty weak right now, but we still believe there's hope for you. We still believe there's hope for you to make the right choices that lead to a better life in the future.*

They kept driving home their point that character would determine my destiny. I just sat there not knowing what to say.

Mrs. Burdick would ask, *"Tom, how are you feeling right now?"* And I'd be like, *"I dunno."* Then she'd say, *"How are you feeling in your heart?"* And I'd be like, *"I dunno! What is this, the Doctor Phil Show? I don't know!!!"*

I didn't know it at the time, but I was using sarcasm to cover up hurts beneath the surface of my life. It was my way of dealing with the pain. I was laughing on the outside, and dying on the inside.

And that was when the Burdicks wrote these words out on a piece of paper:

FEEL - THINK - SAY - DO - HABIT - CHARACTER

They said:

> *Tom, how you feel matters, because that's the beginning of the character process. It starts with how you **feel**. It moves to the way you **think**. When you think about something long enough it comes out in the words you **say**. Over time the things you say become the things you **do**. If you do them long enough they form **habits**... and those habits turn into your **character**.*

I never thought about it that way before, but they were right. And they're still right. Character – who you are when no one's looking – is a never-ending process that happens in all of our lives, making us better or worse.

CHOiCeS

So let me give you the surprising truth I learned along the way. The real power of the character development process is not in the terms themselves; it's in the space between the terms that really matters. The choice between every action – that's what changes everything.

You might not be able to control how you **feel**, but you can control what you **think** about. And when you think about it long enough, you have a choice of what you **say** (and what you choose not to say). From there, you get to choose the things you **do**. And you have a choice of what you do over and over again, and those choices turn into **habits**. Ultimately the habits you choose become the **character** of your life.

This process of character development can essentially be boiled down to the space between each step of the process – the choices you make.

I'm talking about choices like **who influences you**, what music you listen to, what you watch online, who you hang out with, how you handle pain, who you choose to forgive, and the list could go on forever.

What most teens don't realize is that small choices lead to big outcomes over time. Little decisions lead to character strengths or character flaws. Don't believe me? Try chewing on skittles for a month straight and then visit the dentist for a checkup.

And every choice propels you forward toward the life of your dreams or to the life of regret.

What kind of music do you listen to? Could that choice influence who you hang out with? Could it affect who your friends are? Could that choice change where you'll be next weekend? And what if they're not the crowd you should be hanging with? In the heat of the moment could their choices influence you to do something dumb? Something you would regret?

Habits

Many students don't realize how quickly their choices turn into habits, and then they feel stuck because they don't know how to change. They would love to have stronger character, but they have no idea where to start. Even when they really want to change, they just feel lost. The attitude is: *"I'm wish I could be a better person! I guess I'll just do my best and see what happens."* Then they slip back into the same old habits that messed them up to begin with.

As the saying goes, old habits die hard. And that's true: you can't just change your character with the flip of a switch, so you have to look beneath the surface and dive deeper to find the motivation behind your choices. Ask yourself this question:

What **MOTIVATION**…

…is leading to an ACTION…

…that's turning into a HABIT…

…that's becoming my CHARACTER?

Think about what you are struggling with. What bad habits do you want to change? Laziness? Addictions? Blaming? Apathy? (Meaning you just don't care.) Perfectionism? Consumerism? Gossip? Bitterness?

Any bad habit can be changed, but you have to focus on the motivation, not the action itself. You have to find out why you do the things you do.

Psychologists tell us that motivation comes from the expectation of a reward.[14] We are motivated to get a job because we expect a reward: money. We are motivated to make friends with someone because we expect companionship and acceptance, two compelling rewards. We are motivated to get good grades because we expect approval from our parents and because we expect to make the honor role.

That feeling of expectation comes from a naturally occurring chemical in your brain called dopamine.[15] And when your body releases it, you feel awesome – fully alive. It's your happy drug, and man is it addicting.

Here's the catch: you can get a dopamine surge from doing things that are good for you, like laughing with your friends or helping someone out, but you can also get it from doing things that are bad for you, like smoking pot, or getting drunk. You can even get a dopamine surge from bullying people. And the more dopamine you get, the harder it is to break the habit.

So if you want to ditch a bad habit, you have to replace it with something you want more. You have to find the intrinsic motivation to do the right thing, so you can replace the reward you got for doing the wrong thing.

addiction

Your brain loves to memorize the quickest path to a dopamine surge. You want. You need. You take.

Think of your brain like a field of tall grass. The first time you walk through the field toward the reward, you stomp down a few blades of grass. The next time you start to beat down a path. Before long, it's a full-fledged super-highway with no exit to be found. That's how addiction works. Once your brain starts anticipating the reward, you find yourself on that same path again and again, and it becomes almost impossible to stop.

Video games, for example, can be really addicting because they're packed with rewards. You expect small rewards all along the way as you complete each level, and you expect a bigger reward if you beat the game, like having your name listed as one of the top players.

Most of the time with addiction, you're going after a good reward but in the wrong way. In the movie Wreck It Ralph[16], the main character Ralph wants so badly to be appreciated and accepted (he wants a good reward), but he goes about it in the wrong way, ditching his own game, ignoring the rules, and stopping at nothing until he gets the medal. But even when he finally has the medal in his hands, he realizes it doesn't satisfy him. It was nothing more than an empty pursuit.

That's the lie of addiction: that you can find your own shortcut to happiness. Your own secret escape.

It's all promise and no fulfillment.

Addiction is the invisible glass ceiling that will keep you from achieving greatness. It is the chain that will hold you hostage when all you want is to breakthrough.

bREaKTHROUGH (a Poem)

So many people want to break away. Break away from their problems. Break away from their stress. They want to take a break. So they break down before they ever breakthrough. And like a broken record, they break things off before they ever break the cycle.

They wish everyone would just give them a break.

But not you. You want to breakthrough.

So you start breaking down the walls to break new ground. You break the chains, so you can break free. You break the ice to help break the silence. And you break a sweat as you break the mold. But it's worth it. Because you're willing to break your brokenness and break your willpower until at last…

You breakthrough.   (© 2013, by Tom Thelen)

If you can shake off the victim mindset, you really can breakthrough. You're going after a good thing: the desire to find happiness again, to feel normal again, for everything to be alright again.

Just don't go after it in the wrong way.

When you start finding the reward in a positive way, you begin to replace the addiction. You start blazing a new trail through the tall grass in your head. And every time you take the new path, the old one gets more and more overgrown until one day it's unrecognizable.

You broke free.

"It" doesn't own you anymore.

You changed.

○ ○ ○

Take a minute to think about your character and your habits. What are your strengths and weaknesses? Are you struggling with any addictions?

What is holding you back? Seriously.

Every teen has dealt with bad habits and many have felt the pain of addiction, so find some friends with similar goals and setup an accountability group. Invite a trusted adult to be part of it. You need the sage advice of an older soul to help keep you on track. Check in with each other and hold the group to absolute honesty and trust. Together, you can beat this thing.

○ ○ ○

If you really desire to make the right choices – the kind that will turn you into the best version of yourself – then you must commit to making the tough decisions that lead to long term success. Nobody said this journey would be easy. But know this: nothing of great value comes without great sacrifice.

I want you to know I still believe there's hope for any student to make the right choices today that lead to better character tomorrow.

I still believe there's hope for you.

CHAPTER 4 DISCUSSION GUIDE

1. Watch the Victimproof Video Curriculum DVD.
   Createspace.com/372336. Coupon Code: WGU4CUSK

2. On a scale of one to ten, with ten being the best, how would you rate your own character and why?

3. What part of the character process do you need to work on? (feel - think - say - do - habit - character)

4. List at least three small choices you face that will lead to big outcomes over time.

5. How would you describe the connection between dopamine and addiction?

6. What are some of the addictions students at your school are facing?

7. What is one bad habit or addiction you want to break free from?

8. What are some positive rewards you could use to replace that bad habit or addiction?

5. self-esteem

A lot of people think today's teens don't struggle with self-esteem. They've seen the research: American students rate number one in the world for self-esteem.[17] And it's true. But what also means is that students with low self-esteem are surrounded by overconfident peers, leaving them feeling that much more alone and insecure. This is one such story.

So this girl Casie was held back in first grade for spending too much time talking and drawing in class. She enjoyed school, and she was mild mannered, but because she wasn't able to stay on task like the other kids, she was granted another round of first grade.

Casie had the classic "artist personality." And here's the thing about artists: they don't usually thrive in push-down, assembly-line education models. They're much more hands-on. They need to interact and taste life with all of their senses. I could keep explaining how the system didn't work for her, but that's not the point of this chapter. The point is:

Casie was hurt. She was devastated.

I'm not pointing the finger or making her a victim, I'm simply stating the obvious – that kids who are held back in school are burdened with a tremendous load of social and emotional baggage. That baggage often turns to guilt, shame, and insecurity, and over time it comes to define the person. It becomes the limiting factor in the person's life.

At school, kids would say things to Casie. Things like:

… *You're dumb.*

… *You're stupid.*

… *You're not good enough. You'll never be good enough.*

Even as a young kid, the lies began to echo in her head.

I didn't meet Casie until we were both in high school. We met at a local youth group where she played guitar in the band. I had recently started playing guitar, so it was a natural connection. We started hanging out and became good friends. In fact, we became best friends. And about seven years later… Casie and I got married.

Yep. Casie is my wife.

Let me tell you about our first year of marriage. It was back in 2003. I remember becoming increasingly aware of how often Casie would make fun of herself. If she made a little mistake or if she said the wrong thing (like we all do), she would jokingly remark that she was dumb. Sometimes she would even say things like, "Oh my word, I'm so stupid."

Keep in mind, my wife is the most kindhearted person I know. Her greatest strength is building people up. She's a hair stylist, so her whole job is making other people look and feel beautiful. She would never call anyone dumb or stupid, not even as a joke.

But she was making this one exception: for herself.

Over the years the bullies got into her head, and eventually she started to bully herself. There's nothing that wrecks your self-esteem quicker than becoming your own biggest bully.

So I began to notice her saying these things, and it started to hurt. When you're married, you become "one" with the other person, so when they hurt, you hurt too. I found myself not understanding my wife's sarcasm toward herself. I felt like she was holding herself back – like her jokes were affecting her own view of how far she could go in life. So I started remarking back that she's not stupid and she should stop saying things like that.

She agreed, but she didn't stop.

I got more serious about it, and in the months to follow we talked deeper about her past. She knew she wasn't stupid, but she sure joked about it a lot. The whole thing didn't make sense to me because she was such a successful person: a great hair stylist, a wonderful wife, a loyal friend, a volunteer in the community. Everyone just loved her. There was nothing in her life that would have pointed to low self-esteem.

Nothing except... how she treated herself. These jokes. These jokes that felt like tiny knives.

One day I put my foot down:

> *"Stop it honey! You can't call my wife that. I know you're joking, but seriously, you have to stop saying that stuff about yourself. It hurts me, and I think it's hurting you more than you even realize."*

She responded in shock, *"Wow... I didn't even realize I was saying that. Will you help remind me?"*

In that moment she gave me permission. I was put in charge of sticking up for my wife… to my wife. She wanted to stop on her own, but it had become second nature – she didn't even realize she was doing it. So for the next, year any time I heard her say something bad about herself, I would respond, *"Don't call my wife that!"* We wouldn't give up. No one was allowed to call Casie dumb or stupid, not ever herself.

Einstein is credited for saying, "Everybody is a genius. But if you judge a fish by its ability to climb a tree, it will live its whole life believing that it is stupid." [18]

Maybe in your pain, you've begun to believe the lies. Uncovering the hurts of your past is one of the hardest things you will ever do. A lot of people bury it so deep they never go back to revisit it. It's simply too painful.

Many people accept the labels placed on them by society, by their pasts, by their hurts. Casie wasn't the first person to call herself dumb. That wound had been inflicted by bullies at her school, by teachers who didn't understand her learning style, even by family and friends. And because she had never dealt with the pain, she ultimately accepted the lie and lived with the label.

To protect herself from more hurt, she learned to make fun of herself. It's hard for other people to call you dumb when you beat them to the punch. And we all have defense mechanisms like this – things we do to protect ourselves from more pain. Think of the girl who was sexually abused and then never learns to trust people again, or the guy who was cut from the team and decides to never play sports again, or the kid who was bullied and then becomes the bully.

HURT PeoPLe... HURT PeoPLe.

In our hurts, we learn to live with hidden insecurity. We become victims. Our anger turns outward, and we start hurting ourselves and our friends: *You did this to me. It's your fault! You made me do it! If you only knew what it's like to be me!*

Healthy people have the opposite attitude. It's the attitude of I... *I can do this. I am responsible. I am the person who determines how far I can go in life. I may have been hurt in my past, but I'm healing from that.* It's the attitude of personal responsibility.

○ ○ ○

Having low self-esteem will become the limiting factor of your life. But it doesn't have to be that way. It's up to you to break free from your insecurities or to get help from someone who can help you get free.

I found freedom through the Burdick's farm and their intervention in my life. And on the other side of my pain is where I found the greatest purpose for my life. Now my mission is to help other people find that same freedom.

You have to do the same. You have to stop focusing on who hurt you and start focusing on how to get free. That's how you heal from the pain. That's how you turn your pain into a purpose.

Casie has done the same thing. Today, as the owner of her own hair salon, she teaches her employees how to empower other women. Who better to help a woman with pain and insecurity than another woman who is being freed from her own pain and insecurity?

And you have the same opportunity before you. I don't know what baggage you're carrying or who gave it to you, but I know this: if you can accept the freedom of forgiveness, you can discover the purpose for your future. And the greatest purpose of your life is often right on the other side of your pain.

Free People... Free People.

Recently Casie and I were swapping embarrassing stories and she told about her first day in middle school. When the first bell rang, she accidentally ended up in the wrong classroom... surrounded by kids one year ahead of her, many of whom had been her first grade classmates. When the teacher told her she was in the wrong classroom, she was mortified. She left the room completely humiliated, as the other kids made comments that cut like knives. Sometimes Casie still has nightmares where she relives that embarrassing moment. It followed her for decades. And when the memories come back, she forgives again.

You forgive again, so you can live again.

You may find freedom in forgiveness, just as I have, just as Casie did, but you need to remember that forgiveness comes in waves.

You forgive as completely as you can. You give it everything you have, and you find freedom. But then the bitterness tries to creep back in. You discover an old memory and it's like opening up a scar and feeling the wound all over again. What do you do?

You forgive again. And with that forgiveness, you get the gift of being free – free to be fully you.

Free to turn your pain into a purpose.

CHAPTER 5 DISCUSSION GUIDE

1. Watch the Victimproof Video Curriculum DVD. Createspace.com/372336. Coupon Code: WGU4CUSK

2. Why do you think it was so hard for Casie to stop making fun of herself?

3. What are some of the negative effects of having low self-esteem?

4. How you could help someone with low self-esteem?

5. Think of one of the deepest hurts you've experienced. How did it affect your self-esteem?

6. Have you ever felt limited by the hurts of your past? Why or why not?

7. Who do you need to forgive the most and why?

8. What would it look like for you to forgive the people that hurt you the most? (Even if that means keeping your distance from unhealthy people.)

6. Self-discipline

A few years back I volunteered in a mentoring program for at-risk kids. I was placed with student named Jimmy who came from a broken home. He was struggling in school, so we met together once a week for one-hour mentoring sessions. Even with my help, he was still neglecting to do his homework. His teacher had even mentioned to me that she didn't think he had any concept of self-discipline. So the following week I asked him, *"Jimmy, do you know what self-discipline is?"* He sighed and said, *"Sounds like hurting yourself."* And with that he proceeded to jab his pencil right into his leg! I was like, *"Ahhhhh!... Don't do that! Jimmy! Self-discipline is actually a good thing. It's self-correcting to make your own life better."*

Discipline was only a negative term to him.

The reality is: discipline is not something you can avoid. You can either be self-disciplined or you will be disciplined by others. You can self-correct, or you will be corrected by others. It's crazy when you think about it – in America we have a whole department devoted to correcting people who do not correct themselves. It's called the Department of Corrections. Yes, the Department of Corrections – PRISON. It's where you go when you have no self-discipline, so you have to be disciplined by others.

I remember setting the background image on my phone to a picture of me and Jimmy. In the photo he was wearing an orange shirt that said "OUT ON BAIL." It was designed to look like a prison inmate shirt. And every time I looked at my phone, I thought to myself *"That's why I'm doing this – to keep Jimmy from wearing the real life version of that shirt!"*

I always told Jimmy that a sign of maturity is being able to delay satisfaction. In other words, forcing yourself to wait to get something good. You work hard, you stay patient, and ultimately, you earn something valuable through self-discipline. I really wanted him to get it, so I presented him with a crazy choice.

Jimmy, today we can play board games for the first ten minutes, and then do homework for 50 long minutes, OR… we can do homework first for twenty minutes, and play board games for 40 minutes. Which do you choose?

In the first scenario Jimmy would get ten minutes of games, and in the second scenario he would get forty minutes of games. It's a pretty obvious choice right? Not so much. Jimmy could not delay the satisfaction of playing games, so he would choose the ten minutes of instant fun, only to follow it with fifty minutes of grueling homework.

Astonishing. The power of instant satisfaction completely takes over.

○ ○ ○

Many teens struggle with self-defeating behavior. They might choose to spend time on Facebook or YouTube, so they can procrastinate and delay doing their homework. *Why do today what I can put off until tomorrow?* (I should make a bumper sticker of that. I'd become a millionaire for sure.)

And maybe it's becoming your motto. Even if you never say it out loud, are you saying it with your life?

The problem with instant satisfaction is that it breaks down your ability to be self-disciplined. It becomes a distraction. The ten minutes online turns into thirty. By then you've forgotten all about your homework. The thirty minutes turns into a whole evening. Before you know it, you're panicking, slapping together second-rate homework in the class period before it is due.

Problems like this don't go away on their own. They actually grow and fester and turn into monsters that live under your bed and eat little kittens (which are considered a delicacy to monsters).

Each morning when your feet hit the floor, you have a choice. You can feed the monster of procrastination and laziness or you can kick him in the face and ban him from your life. In most cases, a single banning won't do because the monster is so persistent.

Maybe it's all the kittens you've been feeding him.

I'm joking, but there is a lot of truth to that. If you are caught in a cycle of laziness or procrastination, there is really only one way to kill the beast within, and that is with self-discipline.

Self-discipline is the engine that drives character.

Without self-discipline your life drifts into the dark waters of self-destruction. You start to float in any direction except where you actually need to go, and the worst part is that you don't even realize it's happening. You're lost and you don't even know it.

But it doesn't have to be that way.

The key to developing self-discipline is finding something worth living for. Something so valuable, you're willing to kill the lazy monster within.

When I returned home from the Burdick's farm all those years ago, I remember walking into my room and seeing it there – my first electric guitar. My parents knew I had been learning to play, so they bought it for me as a surprise. When I saw it I totally flipped out! I had been learning on my mom's old classical guitar, and this thing was much, much better.

It might only have been a cheap knockoff of a Fender Stratocaster, but it felt like the best guitar in the world. Cause it was mine.

I began practicing every day for hours on end. I used music as a way of releasing all the pent-up emotions I had inside. I finally had a reason to work hard, a reason for some self-discipline.

A few weeks later I formed a band with my friend Brent who played bass, and a couple weeks after that we recruited a guy named Matt to play drums. In the months that followed we enlisted my sister Andrea to sing with me and our friend Dan to play keyboard. We held practice every Saturday from 8am to noon.

I never liked getting up early in on Saturdays in the past, but now it was easy. I knew if we ever wanted to get gigs and make an album, we would need a solid dose of self-discipline to make it happen.

For the next three and a half years we busted our butts for the band. We started by playing free shows for whoever would listen, and over time we began getting paid to play. Before we broke-up and went to college we were getting up to $800 a gig, which was a lot back then. That would be like one million dollars today (well, not quite, but you get the point).

We worked hard using self-discipline to elevate us to new levels as a band. While we were together we saw a lot of other local bands come and go. Some were better musicians than us. Most had nicer instruments than us. But none of them were as focused, as committed, or as disciplined as us. And it showed.

○ ○ ○

For decades, infomercials have advertised weight loss programs that are "quick and easy," claiming things like, "You can have the perfect body in just three minutes a day." The videos are full of smiling skinny people who look like they're having an absolute blast. (Where do they find these people?) Over the years, programs like these came and went, but not many of them caught on.

This was the traditional thinking for weight loss programs: make a program look fun and easy, and people will buy it.

But then something new happened. A guy named Tony Horton started marketing his weight loss program with the complete opposite message. Tony's program was advertised as a 90-day boot camp in your own living room. He was the drill sergeant, and the marketing message was clear: Tony was going to charge you $120 to scream at you through your own TV. He was going to work your own butt off… literally. Guess whose program sold millions of copies and actually worked for millions of people? Yep, Tony's program… more commonly known as P90X.[19]

Not to be outdone, Shaun Thompson ("Shaun T") developed an "insane" workout program that was supposed to be harder than P90X. He claimed it was "the only workout that will leave you face down in a puddle of your own sweat!" (A direct quote from the infomercial.)

A puddle of my own sweat, you say? Yes pleeeease!!!!!

And since Insanity and P90X were both owned by the same company, Beachbody, they shared the same price point. Yes, I'd love to pay you another $120 to scream at me through my own TV.

The crazy thing is: it worked. Many of the same P90X customers shelled out another $120 to get Insanity. Why did it work? The answer is obvious: truth in advertising... the program's claims are true: If you work out until you lay in a pool of your own sweat, YOU WILL LOSE WEIGHT.

People resonated with the P90X and Insanity messages because they knew it was true – the only way to lose weight fast and build muscle is to do an insane workout program. (After this chapter, both of these programs should start sending me a commission check.)

So... truth in advertising: If you want to build character, you have to have self-discipline, but not just with your physical body. You also have to practice self-discipline with your heart and mind. You must take control of your complete being, day after day, week after week.

Sadly, I will not be marketing my own video program to scream at you through your own TV telling you to GET OFF YOUR BUTT AND DO YOUR HOMEWORK!!! PLAN THE BIG EVENT! ASK HER OUT!!! DO SOMETHING AWESOME!

You'll have to tell those things to your**self**. After all, it is called self-discipline for a reason.

You see, self-discipline is not something you choose to do today and it's done. It is not something you can commit to for the next two weeks. No. It is something you choose every day. It's a way of living that says:

> *"I want something so bad I'm willing to kick myself in the butt until I make it happen."*

So how good are you at kicking yourself in the butt? This will be the measure of your self-discipline

CHAPTER 6 DISCUSSION GUIDE

1. Watch the Victimproof Video Curriculum DVD. Createspace.com/372336. Coupon Code: WGU4CUSK

2. Rate yourself on a scale of one to ten, with ten being the best. How are you doing with self-discipline?

3. Name at least one thing you want bad enough that you're willing to work hard to get it.

4. In what area of your life are you having the hardest time with self-discipline?

5. At what times of the day are you most likely to slip into laziness and procrastination?

6. What is one positive step you could take today to improve your self-discipline?

7. CHALLENGE: Get up twenty minutes early tomorrow morning and discipline yourself to do something positive before you go to school. Write out a plan and leave it in an obvious place.

MODULE C

Ending Bullying From The *Outside*-In

7. Honesty

As I gazed out the window the buildings below got smaller and smaller until they disappeared entirely. I was 18, and it was my first time flying. Me, my debate partner Nathan, and our debate coach were headed to Arkansas for a state-wide debate tournament. We had done well in Michigan, we had placed second in Ohio, and now we planned to take Arkansas by storm.

The Arkansas kids talked funny with their southern drawl accents. I remember them saying we had accents too, but I couldn't hear it. They said the Michigan accent was squeaky, like someone talking while pinching their nose. Whatever. We were there to win, not talk about stupid accents. I didn't care if I ever saw these kids again. It was go-time, time to win.

Now, if you've never witnessed a high school debate tournament, it is quite the sight. At the beginning of the school year you are given a debate topic, ours was "Campaign Finance Reform" (exciting, I know). At each debate, you come prepared to argue for either side of the issue, and you don't find out which side until right before the match when the judges flip a coin. It's a lot like the National Football League when you think about it… except for the actual hitting part, and the cheering fans part, and the football part.

So you come prepared to argue for both the affirmative – meaning you say the system should change, or the negative – meaning you want to keep the status quo.

Nathan and I were on a roll, winning debates on either side of the issue. The only challenge was that the local Arkansas teams kept using this one particular quote. The quote was good. The quote was solid. It was from a senator. It was hard evidence, and it was hard to debate against.

The local teams shared the same debate coach, so they all had this same "super-quote" as their prime piece of evidence, and it kept biting us. We knew if we could just find a way to destroy their evidence, we would be invincible, flying our way to the final round with ease. So after the first day of the tournament we searched far and wide for evidence to combat their super-quote. Thanks to Google we found exactly what they were using. We had the whole manuscript. It was from a speech given by some senator on Capitol Hill, but we had nothing to contradict it, no opposite piece of evidence to use against them.

Suddenly, Nathan and I had a bright idea. What if we used selective parts of the quote to make it say what we wanted it to say? We wouldn't jumble the quote or make anything up; we would just stop the quote mid-sentence, so it appeared to be in our favor. We wondered aloud if there was a problem with our plan. Would the judges care if we only used half a quote? The guy still said those words, didn't he? Of course he did, so it was a real quote. End of story. We needed a solution, and we found it.

The next day we made it to the semi-finals before facing super-quote. Out of all the teams in the tournament, we were in the final four, which meant half of the tournament was now watching our debate. We sat behind a small table facing the crowd and a panel of three judges. It was nerve wrecking.

Our opponents came out swinging, presenting a plan so crystal clear it reeked of Windex. And you guessed it, they used the super-quote. It rolled off their tongue like the silver bullet of death.

Super-quote was threatening to undue us. It was kicking us while we were down. Minutes felt like hours as we waited for our turn to speak. Finally, it was time for Operation Half-Quote Trickery. As I approached the podium, I felt a little dishonest, but who had time to think about honesty? We wanted to win. I believe I already established that.

Nathan and I proceeded to use a selection of half-quotes and half-truths to prove our point. And we did a pretty good job of it, to tell you the truth. We were convincing, like real politicians. Everything was going as planned. But what we didn't plan for was about to happen, and that would change everything.

When the other team came up for the questioning round they asked us if we had used half-quotes to mislead the judges. We dodged the question. They asked us if we had purposely ended the quotes mid-sentence to make them portray the opposite meaning. We bumbled out something about how the words we used were actually from the manuscript.

And then it happened… something we didn't expect or even think possible.

The judges actually stopped the debate and asked to see the evidence. Could they even do that? The answer was yes. They were the judges. They could do anything. My heart sank into the souls of my shoes. And even from there I could feel my pulse pounding in my throat.

The judges walked out of the room to review the evidence.

Time.

Stood.

Still.

I wanted to cry. I knew we had been dishonest.

The judges came back in the room and announced that the debate was over. We were immediately disqualified for attempting to deceive the judges.

I was pretty sure they were going to give us the death penalty; send us right to the electric chair. But they didn't. And in seconds, our debate hopes were shattered.

As I raised my head to look up at the judges, I forced myself to say, "You made the right decision."

And they had.

The other team went on to the finals, and we went home disgraced. Completely humiliated.

○○○

It was a high price to pay for a lesson on honesty, but sometimes life has to jolt you awake with the truth.

THERE'S NOTHING LIKE CONSEQUENCES TO HELP YOU UNDERSTAND REALITY.

If I could take back that one moment, I would. I don't mean the moment when we used the half-quote. I mean the moment when we decided to use it... the night before. When we made that one small decision, it was all over from there. I could have stood up for what was right. I could have listened to my conscience. But I didn't. I wanted to win, even if it cost me everything.

Thankfully, I'm not the same person I used to be. I changed, one choice at a time. And a series of right choices leads to right habits, leads to rock solid character.

○ ○ ○

No one likes to think of themselves as a cheater. It's always "the other people" who do the cheating. But the fact is, in the average American high school, 90% of the student population will admit to cheating in a given school year. That means four out of five teens reading this book admit to cheating in school. Are you in the vast majority or the small minority?

The problem with dishonesty is that it breeds more… dishonesty. When you start a lie, it always takes more lies to keep the first one going. And when you justify dishonesty in small things, you will justify it in bigger things down the road.

What kind of a person are you if you cannot be trusted? Trust is like a wall that takes a long time to build up but only a moment to knock down.

Being honest is absolutely worth it. Even if it costs you something big in the short run (like losing a debate or failing a test), it will pay you back in the long run. Honesty will win you the respect of your teachers, the pride of your parents, and the trust of your friends. Students of character know this, and they are proactive about living an honest, trustworthy life.

So how are you doing with honesty? Are you a trustworthy person? Use the study guide on the next page to make a growth plan for this principle.

CHAPTER 7 DISCUSSION GUIDE

1. Watch the Victimproof Video Curriculum DVD. Createspace.com/372336. Coupon Code: WGU4CUSK

2. Why do you think it is so easy to be dishonest?

3. Do you think our society rewards dishonesty?

4. In what area of your life are you having the hardest time with honesty? When is it easiest to be dishonest?

5. How many friends would consider you a trustworthy person? Do you have your parents' trust? What about your teachers? How can you begin to build trust into these relationships?

6. What is one positive step you could take today to improve your honesty and trustworthiness?

7. CHALLENGE: Identify a time when you have been dishonest. Write it down. Now write out a plan to come forth with the truth and make things right.

8. Respect

Darren was 16 when he hacked into the school's grading system. He wasn't trying to give himself all A's. He was simply trying to prove a point. He changed the scores for one single test; it was a history exam that every kid in class thought was too difficult and unfair. He didn't just change his grade; he gave perfect scores to all his friends – a regular Robin Hood of the computer hacking world. Things were going great until he got caught. He and his friends received failing grades and a temporary vacation from school. Even worse, they lost the **respect** of their parents and teachers.

When Darren told me this story, it was clear that the root problem was not the dishonesty of his crime (to be clear, that was a problem, just not the biggest problem). Darren's cheating was only an outer sign of an inner problem. Darren's problem was respect. Or to put it more clearly, disrespect. He didn't care what the teachers thought, what his parents would think, or what the consequences were. He wanted to stick it to the man and make a public point that the test was unfair. He had absolutely no appreciation for all the work and all the dedication the teacher put in day after day. He wanted to put the teacher in his place.

Darren wasn't a punk kid; he was a disrespectful kid. The core virtue behind respect is valuing all lives and appreciating all the people who came before us, whose shoulders we now stand on. It is being grateful for every advantage we are born into and for every privilege we are given.

Respect is accepting the debt of gratitude and honor that we owe the world even when we don't feel like it.

When I speak at schools I often ask for a show of hands for how many people know the first name of one of the custodians in their school. If 10% - 20% of the audience raises their hands, it's a good day. Even in the best cases, the vast majority of students do not know the first name of a single janitor in their school. Why is that?

The quick answer is we do not respect what we do not know. The more complicated answer is we make assumptions about people based on their job, clothes, hair, skin color, voice, you name it. We group these assumptions into categories called "stereotypes." Think about how society, television, and the internet stereotype the janitor profession. The unsaid message is that janitors are not smart, not interesting, not clean, and not worth talking to.

Even with the disrespect that surrounds professions like custodians, lunch ladies, fast food workers, and trash collectors, they still willingly serve us day-in and day-out cleaning up the puke in the cafeteria, serving us French Fries, and picking up the trash at the curb.

What kind of assumptions are you making about the people who fly under the radar of your life? What about the people who have authority in your life, like teachers and parents?

It's easy to respect people who are just like us. We hang out with the same friends, we like the same bands, we dress the same, we look the same. But it is more difficult to respect the unknown – people who are different than us. The cool thing is: when we get to know people, we find out that we have much more in common than we originally thought. Although we humans have vast differences on the outside, we share huge similarities on the inside. We face the same fears, battle the same insecurities, have the same hopes, and dream the same dreams. We all want our lives to matter.

As a teen, that didn't click with me. I didn't respect my teachers until they earned it, and I assumed they were doing the same for me. Since I had no respect for myself, I had almost none for anyone else. It was a vicious cycle that led me down a dark path. Thank God I am not the person I used to be.

So what changed?

When I was on the Burdick's farm they taught me that I would only get as much respect as I gave to others. Since I gave none, I received none in return. I remember being late one morning as I was getting ready for school, and Mr. Burdick let me have it. He said:

> Son, you are not being respectful of Mrs. Burdick's time. When you are late, it's like telling the other person that your time is more important than their time! Do you do this to your mother at home? Your mother went into the bowels of death to bring you to life, so you owe nothing less than your utmost respect and honor.

At the time I thought he was being a bit overdramatic (what with the "bowels of death" and everything), but over time, his comments rang true. My parents don't have to earn my respect; I owe it to them by default. The same goes for any person of authority.

The key is understanding when respect is due and how respect is earned. As a student, you give respect to others but you earn it for yourself.

THAT'S NOT FAIR, you say?

Yep, you're right, it's not fair. But respect isn't built on fairness. Respect is built on accepting the debt of gratitude and honor that you owe this world for the gift of life itself.

CHAPTER 8 DISCUSSION GUIDE

1. Watch the Victimproof Video Curriculum DVD. Createspace.com/372336. Coupon Code: WGU4CUSK

2. Rate yourself on a scale of one to ten, with ten being the best. How are you doing with respect toward your parents, teachers, friends, and even to yourself?

3. In the last week where have you been the most respectful? Teachers, Parents, Yourself? Where have you struggled with disrespect?

4. Give yourself a do-over. Think of a recent time when you were disrespectful, and write what you will do differently in the future.

5. Write down one relationship in your life where respect is due and another one where it is earned. What are some of the differences you see?

6. CHALLENGE: Find the person(s) you were disrespectful to and offer a sincere apology. Let them know you're working on being more respectful, and do something kind for them to show your sincerity.

9. Responsibility

Responsibility is an easy word to figure out. Response-ability: it's your ability to respond. Your response is your responsibility.

As long as you're alive, you always have the ability to respond. When you're dead you lose this ability. I guess you could say dead people are completely irresponsible… because they're dead. So until you die, you own your response. It's your responsibility.

If you take one thing away from this chapter, take this:

own your Life.

This is the essence of responsibility.

The opposite of being a victim isn't being a bully. The opposite of being a victim is being an owner. An owner is someone who takes responsibility for their choices and actions. Even when they mess things up, they don't make excuses. They own it.

Recently I was watching the news and a group of reporters were badgering this military general. They were peppering him with questions about some breach of intelligence somewhere overseas. I barely even remember what it was about because I was stunned by the general's response. The reporters pushed harder, *"Whose fault is this? Who is* **responsible** *for this massive breach of security?!!"*

The general stopped, looked right at them, and said in a calm voice, "You're looking at him. I am."

Whaaa??? He just sat there and took responsibility for the whole thing? Unreal. I mean, there were so many other excuses he could have made. The general wasn't the actual person who messed up. It was obviously an officer under him – probably several levels under him. I bet he didn't even know who did it, but he stood there and took full responsibility. On live TV. Before the whole world.

It left the reporters speechless.

He owned it.

"It wasn't my fault!" "I had no choice!" It is much more common to hear this kind of language. These are the slogans of "victims" who know nothing of responsibility. It's as if outside forces are responsible for all the bad things that happen in their life. They certainly aren't responsible for it – they are the victims of it.

When things go good, they're the first to take credit, but when things go bad, they're the last to accept blame.

They become professional blame-shifters. When blame shows up on their front porch, they simply move to a different house. Let's just shift this blame over here, over there, anywhere! Blame is a hot potato that many people cannot handle because they simply refuse to own it.

Students who refuse to own their lives end up making excuses for everything. Sometimes it gets pretty silly, as they shift the blame to anyone but themselves.

Take homework, for example. Over the years I've collected homework excuses and put them in my list of the top ten homework excuses of all time.

See if any of these excuses sound familiar to you…

Top Ten Homework Excuses:

1. My dog ate my homework (aka "The Classic").

2. I have a solar powered calculator, so I couldn't do my homework last night. It was too dark.

3. Timmy fell into a lake, so I jumped in to rescue him! …Sadly my homework drowned.

4. I accidentally dropped my homework in the toilet, and somehow it got flushed.

5. I gave my homework to a homeless man to line his hat with – for warmth.

6. The internet was down, my computer crashed, and the printer broke all at the same time!

7. My great aunt died last night, so we spent the rest of the night planning her funeral.

8. I made a paper airplane out of my homework, but it got hijacked.

9. I put my homework in the safe, but I lost the combination.

10. My little brother threw up all over my homework… It was nasty.

Some of these excuses might have even happened to you. Perhaps your little brother actually did puke on your homework. Whose responsibility is that? Did he take you hostage and demand to use your homework as his barf-bag? I'm hoping the answer to that is no. If the answer is yes, then you have more problems than being irresponsible. Also, your brother needs some Pepto-Bismol.

○ ○ ○

T*PS and TR*CKS

As a student, one of your main responsibilities is to do your homework. Here are some tips and tricks for getting it done and turning it in on time.

The default temptation is to try to remember everything in your head. For example, throughout the school day, you are assigned homework in math, science, and history. You try to remember the list in your head, then you find yourself panicking the next day at school when you realize you totally forgot.

My first tip is to get that list out of your head into a place where it can be collected.

In his book, Getting Things Done[20], David Allen describes this as a "bucket." If something is important but cannot be completed in two minutes or less, then you put it into your bucket. Obviously we're not talking about a literal bucket; we're talking about creating a place for collecting all your upcoming assignments and appointments. This could be a notebook, a computer, or even a handheld device like a phone or an iPod. Many schools provide students with a planner or a calendar for this very use. Any assignment that cannot be done immediately gets collected in your bucket.

TIP 1: Get a bucket and begin collecting all your assignments in it.

TIP 2: Set an alarm.

The key to Tip 2 is to setup an auto-reminder for what's in your bucket. You can leave your backpack by the door as a reminder, put a piece of paper on your pillow, tie a string on your finger, or even write something on your hand! You can go high-tech and set a reminder on your phone, computer, or iPad. The sky is the limit, so find what works for you.

Responsibility means being honest with yourself and setting a reminder before you forget... because you know you will forget.

Here's how I do it. My bucket is my notebook and my computer. The first question I ask myself is: "Can I do this in the next two minutes?" If the answer is yes, I do it immediately and get it out of the way (so I don't even collect it in my bucket). If the answer is no, then it goes in one of two places. Anything I need to get done today goes in my notebook on my list of tasks for the day. Everything else goes into my online calendar. I even setup auto-reminders to pop up before the events are due. For smaller tasks (things that take less than an hour) I set a popup reminder for the night before.

The point is: get it out of your brain and into your bucket, then setup a reminder for your bucket. What I love about this method is that it allows me to forget about it! This is a huge stress reliever. The bucket remembers for me, so I don't have to.

Let's face it: homework can be about as much fun as giving your eye a paper cut, but only one of those things will hurt you. So if you're unsure, try them both and get back to me. If you find yourself blaming everyone else for everything else in your life, then it's time to start taking responsibility. Your attitude must be, "If I don't like my current situation, then it is up to me to make it better."

The world is full of excuse-makers and buck-passers, but a responsible person is hard to find. If you can learn to accept responsibility for your choices, your actions, and your happiness, you will become something very valuable and rare... a person who truly owns their life.

CHAPTER 9 DISCUSSION GUIDE

1. Watch the Victimproof Video Curriculum DVD. Createspace.com/372336. Coupon Code: WGU4CUSK

2. What are some of the excuses you've heard people use for not turning in their homework?

3. Rate yourself on a scale of one to ten, with ten being the best. How are you doing with responsibility?

4. In what areas of your life are you most likely to be irresponsible?

5. If you were put on the spot for missing a homework assignment, what would be your natural response? Accept the blame, shift the blame, make excuses, or maybe disappear?

6. What is one positive step you could take today to take charge of your life and to be an owner?

7. CHALLENGE: Next time you are held responsible for something, make absolutely no excuses. Accept the blame and take full responsibility.

MODULE D

Leading The Anti-Bullying Revolution

10. PURPOSE

Have you ever met people who constantly retell the same old jokes and stories from back in the day? It's almost like their best days are behind them, way back in their glory days. Or maybe you've seen people do just the opposite: they sit around daydreaming about their future stardom, waiting to be discovered. It's like they're living in a future fantasy world.

A lot of people get stuck living too far in the future or in the past, and they miss out on the here and now.

I remember when I was about twelve I wanted nothing more than to be a teenager. From what I heard, this would be the best time of my life. My Dad and I were working in our Christmas tree field one afternoon, and we paused to take a breather. I was daydreaming about becoming a teen and driving and having a girlfriend and all of that, when I asked my Dad what was the best time in his life. I was thinking he would say when he was sixteen, or maybe when he was eighteen. I wanted him to confirm that the teen years were the best. So I asked him straight out.

He paused for a second, leaned into his shovel, and said with certainty,

"...PROBABLY RIGHT NOW."

The way he said it was so riveting, so resolute, that I knew he meant it. If you would have heard his voice, there was no "probably" about it. And in those few words, my Dad imparted a worldview that sticks with me to this day. I remember these words when I start living in the future or in the past. And it's in these moments that I stop. I breathe. And I whisper to myself, "...Probably right now."

Right now is the time to start finding your purpose in life. When you can learn to value your current reality, you will start to become fully present. Your eyes will open up to a bigger world, and you'll begin seeing problems as opportunities to grow.

As a student, one of your biggest opportunities is to discover your unique purpose – to figure out what role you play in the ANTI-BULLYING REVOLUTION.

A common idea about finding your **PURPOSE** is that it's made up of three parts: mission, vision, and values.[21]

MISSION answers the question of HOW. *How are you going to carry out your purpose?*

VISION tells us WHAT you want to achieve. *What do you want to accomplish with your purpose?*

VALUES answers the questions of WHY. *Why is the purpose important to you? What do you believe in?*

People say it all the time: *"You gotta discover your mission-vision-values!",* and usually in that order. Corporations spend boatloads each year to identify their mission-vision-values.

Here's the problem: They got it all wrong. Well not "wrong" exactly. They actually got it backwards.

If you start with the HOW (the Mission), and then move on to the WHAT and WHY, it's easy to get discouraged and give up. Each of us has a core need to *first* identify what's important to us. We have to discover *why we want to do what we want to do.* The WHAT and the HOW come later.

As a student, you are at the best stage of life to experiment and take risks until you discover your unique purpose. Identifying your strengths and weaknesses now while you're young is what propels you forward toward your purpose.

○ ○ ○

Recently I spoke at youth conference in Oregon. After my speech the students broke into small groups for a time of discussion. Since my flight wasn't leaving until later that night, I had time to stick around and join a few of the groups. One of the students, who I'll call Jeff, was having a hard time answering the question of **why**. He was hung up on the values question: *What is important to you? What do you value?*

Since he was tongue tied, I tried to help out. *"Jeff, what is something that's valuable to you? What do you care about?"* I said. After several moments of awkward silence, he finally replied in a quiet voice, *"Food."* That was all he said: food. I almost thought he was joking, but he wasn't laughing. I prodded further: *"Okay, cool. Tell me more about food. What do you mean by that?"*

He went on to describe how the food at his school was terrible. It was unhealthy and over-processed with no nutritional value. It turns out that Jeff was an aspiring chef, but no one at his school knew it. He was too afraid to admit it. But once he got past his fears, he discovered his **why**, and the group moved on to help identify the **what** and **how**.

The students brainstormed about holding a "healthy snack day" at school. They dreamed up a team he could form to help carry out the vision. They even proposed that his group could make a presentation before the school board, asking for funding to bring healthy food choices back to their cafeteria.

Jeff discovered his *why*, and from there his *what* and *how* became very clear.

○ ○ ○

So why do so many students fail to find their "why?" Most of the time it's because they fail to go through this experimentation phase. They're too afraid to fail, they stop taking risks and wait around for the world to discover how great they are.

A lot of people believe that life is a stage, and each one of us is the star in our own play about us. And it almost seems true because when you think about it, for pete's sake, you are in every scene! Everywhere you go, there you are. You must be the star, right?

The trouble with this philosophy is that it leads to a self-centered, self-focused, self-ish life. You get a thrill when your life is going good, but when your plans fall apart (as all peoples' plans do from time to time) your life falls apart. You become the victim.

111

wHen Life is aLL abouT youR stoRy, iT ends uP being a veRy smaLL stoRy indeed.

People who know their purpose are not like this. They take life as a gift. They see each day as a new opportunity to play a part in a greater story. A story bigger than self... now that is a grand concept. So how do you go from being a person who doesn't care to someone who really cares?

Answer: By putting others first. What do I mean by that? Do I mean giving up the best piece of chicken, so your little sister can have the drumstick? Do I mean letting other people go first in line? Do I mean putting away your iPad to spend time with grand-mama? Yes, I mean all of these things.

Caring is cultivated by small choices made over a lifetime, but taking that initial step (to put others first) can seem counterintuitive to our human nature. What about me? Who's looking out for me? Don't feel bad, that question is common to humanity. It's in our default settings.

I never had to teach my kids to say *"Mine!"* I never sat them down and said, *"Listen, here's what I want you to do: I want you to cry whenever you're hungry and scream when you're poopy."* No one has to teach this stuff because we're naturally wired to get our own needs met. But as we grow older, learning to recognize and meet the needs of others becomes the key ingredient to maturity. Becoming others-focused is an essential ingredient to becoming who you were meant to be. In his book, Blue Like Jazz[22], Donald Miller calls it *"discovering that other people exist."* This act of caring for others is what makes us fully human. It's what separates us from the animals.

Side Note: This is a great line to use on your best friend Bob. Next time Bob does something awkward at the lunch table (it could be anything, doesn't matter), just remark, *"Bob! Come on! That's the one thing the separates us from the animals!"* Bob will love this, I assure you.

Back to caring. People of purpose choose to care even when they don't feel like it. I don't always feel like caring, but when I force myself to do it, the feeling of satisfaction follows. If I wait for my emotions to lead the way, I will end up lying on the couch every night watching reruns of UFC while the world goes to you-know-where in a hand basket. So I kick myself in the butt and volunteer at the food bank, serve at the nonprofit organization, plan the neighborhood block party, and change my kids' diapers (and let me tell you as a father of twins, that is no small task).

Life is far too great to be lived in selfishness.

You owe it to the world to discover your purpose. We need you to become fully alive to your unique contribution. You will never get there by sitting on the sidelines of life. Instead, you have to get up off the couch and start trying new things. You have to experience real failure and real success to find clarity in your purpose... a purpose greater than self.

So when should you start testing your skills, risking your pride, and exploring this question of *why?*

Probably right now.

CHAPTER 10 DISCUSSION GUIDE

1. Watch the Victimproof Video Curriculum DVD. Createspace.com/372336. Coupon Code: WGU4CUSK

2. How can you tell when someone is living too much in the past or too much in the future?

3. Why is it backwards to identify your Purpose through the process of Mission-Vision-Values?

4. What are some of the fears that keep students from discovering their purpose?

5. What is one thing that is really important to you and why? *(Identify your VALUES – the why.)*

6. What does your preferred future look like? What are you going to change? *(Identify your VISION–the what.)*

7. How, specifically, could you bring that vision to reality? *(Identify your MISSION – the how.)*

11. Teamwork

So you're in an awkward group setting with a bunch of new people, and the leader starts out by saying, *"Let's all go around the room and say our name and one interesting thing about ourselves."* Or maybe the leader wants you to say something you're good at, or tell about your hobbies. This is called the "ice breaker." It's a game designed to put the group at ease and relieve the obvious tension in the room. The paradox is that the ice breaker actually starts out by achieving the opposite goal - it makes people feel more anxiety and more awkwardness, as they wait for their turn to speak.

The room is quiet and awkward as people start giving their mini-speeches. Just remember that no one will remember what you're about to say... because they're too busy thinking about what they're going to say when it's their turn, and then they're analyzing what they just said when their turn is over. This isn't necessarily a good or a bad thing. It's just how the game works.

You will notice that most people start out by taking their turn in as little time as possible. They just want to get the spotlight off them. This is like my wife: she doesn't like it when a group of people stares at her. And most people are this way. But the thing is, what the group really needs is for someone to pop the balloon, letting all the hot air and tension out of the room. Everyone is drowning in awkwardness until you do it, so you take it upon yourself to serve the group in this way.

It will be best to sit about halfway around the circle, right across from the group leader, so that your turn comes in the middle, when the tension is at its highest. You're not looking to get attention - you just want to help the group by breaking the ice of the ice breaker.

HERE ARE MY TOP FIVE WAYS TO "BREAK THE ICE' OF THE ICE BREAKER:

1. Say, *"I'm Tom Thelen, and I do Imagination Magic. I tell people to close their eyes and imagine a piece of rope. Then imagine me cutting the rope in two. Now imagine I just put the rope back together into one solid piece. Viola! Open your eyes!... Imagination Magic!"* (Don't actually have them close their eyes; just describe to how you do your Imagination Magic. This is key.)

2. Introduce yourself as the person sitting next to you, the person whose turn is coming right after yours. Then act embarrassed, like you didn't mean to say that. (Note: this only works if you already know the name of the person sitting next to you.)

3. Say, *"I'm Tom Thelen, and one thing I'm good at is paint stirring. If someone has a can of paint that needs stirring, I'm all over it. I've been doing this since I was a small child, and I have become highly skilled in this regard."*

4. Say, *"I'm Tom Thelen, and one thing people don't know about me is that I have only four toes on my left foot ... Motorcycle accident. It's really hard for me to talk about."* If people ask to see the foot, just run out of the room screaming like you're having a flashback.

5. Don't say anything at all. Instead, just shoot small fireworks out of your hat. *(Note: you will need to acquire a hat that shoots small fireworks.)*

The point is: it's not good for a group of people to sit silently in a room feeling shy, anxious, and awkward. We need someone besides the "actual leader" to say, *"I'm not willing to let that happen. Not on my watch."* Then we need that person to make us laugh - even at their expense. All the group really wants is to know that they're in a safe place and that everything is going to be okay. So even while we're laughing at you, you should know that we are all silently grateful for your kind act of self-sacrifice.

The truth is: you're actually hoping that some other brave soul will do it before you have to. Because you know that if the room is still full of hot air when the spotlight finally gets to you, you will be the one to pop the balloon. This is your calling…

YOU'RE AN ICE BREAKER BABY.

○ ○ ○

Part of leading the Anti-Bullying Revolution is learning how to work with a team. Teamwork depends highly on the dynamics of the group – how the team interacts. In the 1960s a 27-year old professor from Ohio State University wrote an article that forever changed how the world would view group dynamics. His name was Bruce Tuckman. Tuckman maintained that every group goes through four stages of development: **forming, storming, norming, and performing.**[23]

FORMING

In the forming stage, the group is testing the waters and getting to know each other; it's like a first date. And as the team roles become official, the group solidifies and enters a sort of honeymoon phase. Like most honeymoons, this phase is very short lived, and everything goes great. There is a lot of good will amongst the team members. It's fun. People are excited about the possibilities of the group.

In this phase, make sure to involve everyone in the decision making process. Leadership guru Stephen Covey is famous for saying "Without involvement, there is no commitment."[24] In other words, you must involve your team and hear everyone's voice if you want their full commitment and energy. If you can move forward with consensus, you can develop the stamina to weather the "storm" of the next stage.

STORMing

The storming stage cannot be avoided – every successful group goes through it, so do not be alarmed. In this stage, the group members start competing for power and influence. They begin debating which ideas are best for moving forward.

You can see how easily the group dynamics will change from Kumbaya around the campfire (forming stage) to *"My ideas are better than yours!!!"* (storming stage).

Inside Tip: Watch your blind spots. Sometimes group members have a "hidden agenda" or an unsaid goal they're trying to achieve. Perhaps a group member has something to gain if you take a certain action. Maybe their agenda is to get money or power or whatever. It will be very hard to build a unified team if someone is operating with a hidden agenda. Don't get paranoid, but be diligent and explain the importance of being real, honest, and up front with everything.

When your group is storming, stamina is key. Hang in there. Don't get emotionally involved in your ideas. Don't make them "your baby." When everyone gets possessive about their ideas, the group often gives in to the person who shouts the loudest.

Conflict can actually be a very healthy thing for the group, as long as you go through it with respect.

norming

If you can find ways to value the contribution of each member, the group can ease into the norming stage. Publically acknowledge each member's and ideas, even if the group will ultimately go in another direction. Don't be fake, but genuinely seek diverse opinions.

Insecure leaders build consensus by surrounding themselves with yes-men. They quickly arrive at the norming stage, only to find themselves surrounded by mediocrity. Yes-Men (or Yes-Women) agree with whatever the leader says. They are too self-conscious to have a difference of opinion. So the group slogs through at the pace of the control freak leader. You end up with a low performing, dysfunctional group.

Not so with you. You want to reach a legitimate norming stage the old fashioned way, so you work through your problems, you build consensus, and you stress the team's goals over individual pet projects.

Be proactive and encourage the group to get all their ideas out during the meetings (no meeting-after-the-meeting in the hallway). Tell them you subscribe to the iron-sharpens-iron principle and you value good, healthy conflict. When conflict is handled with mutual respect, it can actually produce some of the best ideas.

PerFormin8

As the group's purpose becomes clear, you can gain momentum to move into the performing stage. In this stage the group becomes a well-oiled machine.

To make it to the highest level of group development, you must **build trust** and **pour vision** back into your team! With a foundation of trust and a clear understanding of the vision, the team's performance level can go through the roof!

○ ○ ○

Have you ever noticed there is a big difference between having the title of "leader" and being the actual leader of a group? We all know who the official leader is, but who is the unofficial leader? Who has the most influence in the group? I call this being the "perceived leader." What do I mean by that?

If a group of aliens observed your group and couldn't understand one word that was said, who would they say the leader is? Who would they perceive to be the leader? In the best groups, the official leader is also the perceived leader, but in many teams this is not the case. You can see it in the eyes of the group members. Who captures every eye in the room when they talk? Who does everyone look at during the critical moments? Most of the time, this person is the perceived leader. Like it or not, the perceived leader is the most influential person in the room. That doesn't mean they're always the loudest, the most talkative, or the most prepared. But when they speak, everyone listens. Perceived leadership isn't given by title, or won through elections. It is earned over time through building relationships and producing results.

○ ○ ○

Jessica was Student Council President, a title she had won decisively in the school election. She was well prepared and focused for the student council meetings, but other than having the support of the Treasurer (her best friend Alison), she could not gain traction with the rest of the team. After one meeting, she noticed a couple of team members having a sidebar conversation (also known as a "meeting after the meeting"). They were second guessing a decision the group had made during the meeting. This made Jessica very frustrated, and she wanted to quit. Why wouldn't they voice their concerns during the meeting? Why wouldn't they support the groups' decision over their own agenda?

These questions echoed through her brain.

Jessica was the official leader, but she wasn't the perceived leader of the group… at least not yet.

In my experience, there are four levels of leadership that every leader must move through with their group to achieve the highest level of success. These unseen levels of leadership are the keys to victory or defeat with any team. Leaders who consistently climb the levels, bringing their teammates with them along the way, achieve real success with their group.

LEADERSHIP BY RIGHTS:

The first level is what I call "Leadership by Rights." In Jessica's case, she is the official Student Council President. She alone holds the rights to that office. She has the right to schedule meetings, to make the agenda, and to set the course of action for the school year. She can even invoke these rights by demanding that her team follows her. But if she demands her rights as the leader, what will happen? Most likely she will accomplish the exact opposite goal – her teammates will either quit, revolt, or follow her with bad attitudes. In the real world, Leadership By Rights doesn't get you very far. You know why? Because I'm the boss, that's why! I'm the boss, and you can follow me or lose your job. Blah blah blah. No one wants to follow this kind of leadership for obvious reasons, but they do so for fear of being fired, embarrassed, or kicked off the team.

LEADERSHIP BY RELATIONSHIPS:

The second level is Leadership by Relationships. Jessica's best friend is Alison, the Student Council Treasurer. To Alison, Jessica is more than the President of the Student Council; she is also a true friend. There is no mystery to why the one girl follows the other. Alison and Jessica have a great relationship, so they make great teammates. The second level of leadership says that if people like you (and more importantly, if they know you like them), then they will follow you. In school elections, this can sometimes be the deciding factor behind who wins the race and who goes home defeated. The underlying belief is that people who like us will make decisions that are in our best interests. We trust you. You are a friend.

The danger at this level is that some leaders get stuck in relationship mode, and they cannot move beyond it. They try to please all the people all the time, so they change their views with the pulse of popular opinion. They become like politicians who are forever running for office. Ironically, this is what erodes trust in their team, the very thing they are trying so hard to build.

LEADERSHIP BY RESULTS:

A high level leader learns to take the team beyond the relationship level by adding the third level of leadership: Leadership by Results. In this level, the teammates begin to trust the track record of the leader. They see all the hard work and all the discipline, and it proves to them that the leader has the group's best interests at heart, even when it is unpopular.

Leadership by Results is risky business. You have to be secure enough to make the tough call, to cast the tie-breaking vote, and to stand firm when necessary. Along the way, you learn that real success cannot be attained without risking real failure. I would even go further, saying that real success is only obtained by walking through real failure.

LEADERSHIP BY RESPECT:

But here's the cool part. When you lead by relationships and by results, you can eventually be propelled into the highest level of leadership: Leadership by Respect. Again, you've been bringing your team with you along the way. They like you, and they like your results, so they begin to trust your judgment. They begin to respect you as a leader, and that means they will value your opinions and contributions even when they disagree with you. To be clear, it doesn't mean they will always agree with you, but it means they will always respect you.

In the first level, you are given rights, and people follow you if they have to. In the second level, you build relationships, and people follow because they believe you have their personal best interests at heart. In the third level, you start to develop a track record of good results, and people follow because they believe you have the best interests of the team in mind. And in the final level, people follow you because they respect you, trusting that you have everyone's best interests at heart.

Now for the special sauce. Did you notice that you can do levels two, three, and four without ever being given the official title of "leader? "It's true. And this is the challenge that 95% of leaders find themselves in. They want to lead, but they don't have the official title. The temptation is to sit back and be quiet until someone calls on you. The temptation is to be passive-aggressive. The temptation is to have a meeting after the meeting, or to say things like, "Well, I wouldn't have done it that way."

The reality is this. We need unofficial leaders to speak up. We need perceived leaders to step up. We need team players who will shoulder the load of leadership and serve the group over their own special interests.

Remember: as the leader, you are the glass ceiling. You set the expectations, the mood, and the dynamics.

Victims pass the buck. Victims play mind games with people. But not you. You're a leader. And if you really want your team to work, **you are responsible** to continually focus on teamwork.

CHAPTER 11 DISCUSSION GUIDE

1. Watch the Victimproof Video Curriculum DVD. <u>Createspace.com/372336</u>. Coupon Code: WGU4CUSK

2. Have you ever had to "break the ice of the icebreaker? How did you do it? / How would you?

3. Of the Four Levels of Leadership, which two levels help you achieve level four, Leadership By Respect?

4. Why do you think so many groups fall apart when they get to the "norming" stage?

5. Why do you think people try so hard to avoid conflict? Can conflict ever be a good thing?

6. What is one positive step you can take today to build teamwork in your group?

7. CHALLENGE: Next time your group has a conflict, encourage them to work through it with respect. Explain the importance of healthy conflict.

12. Leadership

Fifty years ago a small group of young people made a decision that resulted in huge cultural changes across the United States. They decided to stand up for what they believed in – the principle that all people should be treated equally, a principle known as civil rights.

These young people would come to be known as The Freedom Riders[25], but at the moment, they were just ordinary young people and college students. They were normal kids who went to class each day, did their homework each night, and dreamed that one day their lives would mean something.

When you think about the civil rights time table, this story doesn't seem to fit in with everything else. It had been nearly 100 years since slavery had been outlawed.

Nearly 100 years since the remaining 40,000+ slaves were set free. Nearly 100 years since so many of them took on new last names, like Freeman or King (because they were free men who felt like kings).

But consider the timetable. In 1863 Lincoln gives his famous Emancipation Proclamation speech and declares all slaves free.[26] Two years later, in 1865, Congress passes the Thirteenth Amendment outlawing slavery. Two years between the speech and the law. That's a long time. The wheels of politics turn slowly. But how slow do the wheels of society turn?

Much. Much. Slower.

Two years between the speech and the law, and for the next 100 years black people remain subject to the most shameful, dehumanizing treatment in the United States: separate drinking fountains for whites and "coloreds," separate bathrooms, segregated schools, whites-only restaurants, flaming crosses, and death by hanging for innocent black men and women.

It was social cruelty – bullying on a massive scale.

Slavery may have ended in 1863, but a hundred years later the echoes could still be heard loud and clear. The chains of slavery had been broken, but the shadows and scars remained. In the 1960s, African Americans had legal rights, but they were far from having civil rights.

The Supreme Court eventually stepped in with laws to end the discrimination, and in 1960 they outlawed racial segregation on public transportation busses, terminals, and restaurants. But even after the law was in place, blacks were still being mistreated and abused in these very same places.

One group had enough. In Washington DC, a black leader named James Farmer organized a group calling itself CORE - The Congress of Racial Equality.[27] Farmer decided it was time to take action. So he recruited groups of blacks and whites to test the new laws by riding public busses into the deep south. They would boldly face discrimination and perhaps even violence on their journey toward racial reconciliation.

Like Dr. Martin Luther King Jr., the Freedom Riders would embrace a philosophy of nonviolence, committing to turn the other cheek and to never return violence for violence.

What followed was more than anyone expected. Local police organized violent attacks with the Ku Klux Klan in Anniston and Birmingham Alabama. When the Freedom Riders arrived at the public bus station in Anniston, they were met by an angry mob. The bus driver tried to pull away, but the mob slashed the tires, lit the bus on fire, and held the doors shut trying to burn them alive.

Local police stood by watching it happen… and they did absolutely nothing to stop it.

When the bus's fuel tank exploded, the mob moved back, and the Freedom Riders poured out of the bus, gasping and choking for air. But before they could get away, the mob moved back in and beat many of them to a bloody pulp until highway patrolmen fired warning shots into the air, and the mob scattered.

The riders received minimal medical treatment before being kicked out of the local hospital, and they continued on to Birmingham, Alabama, where they were met with more violence. They continued on despite the very real threat that in every city, large mobs of ignorant white supremacists would try to kill them.

You would think this level of violence would have sent them packing their bags, heading home for safety. But in fact, it did just the opposite. More Freedom Rides started up at college campuses and churches in the northern states. And facing brutal beatings, false imprisonment, and even death, the rides continued on.

Hundreds of riders were arrested and sent to jail in Jackson Mississippi, until the jails literally filled up. And all this not for breaking the law, but for exercising their legal rights to a civil society where blacks and whites are treated as equal. And guess what? It worked.

The Freedom Riders became known for breaking down some of the most hateful discrimination in American history. All because they decided to stand up and lead.

Let's go back to the night that James Farmer recruited the first group of Freedom Riders. Whether the students in the room knew it or not, each of them was living their life in one of four ways: as a wanderer, explorer, follower, or leader. That night, they were challenged to become followers of a great vision. A vision to end racism.

The same holds true today. In your school, in your class, on your team, and all around you, people live as wanderers, explorers, followers, and leaders.

wanderers

Wanderers are people who have no purpose. They lack the motivation to serve anyone but themselves. Drifting through life without ambition or determination, they fail to see past the present moment. They are unaware of the needs of others, and they live to gratify the immediate desires of their own existence.

Wanderers might talk about their ambitions, but their daydreams never come to fruition, as they wait for life to reward them for doing, well… nothing. Some of you are like, "Listen Buddy: playing 5 hours of video games a night isn't nothing! It's an accomplishment!" Uhmm yeah. Keep telling yourself that. While you occupy the couch, the rest of us will be taking ambition, being the change, and rocking the world.

The thing is: most wanderers don't even know they're wandering. They don't know they're missing out on a greater story. They "don't know what they don't know," so they become stuck in perpetual childhood, wandering through life with no purpose.

Fortunately for you, if you've read this far, you are probably already searching for more in life, and that kind of searching is what makes you an explorer.

EXPLORERS

Explorers are searching for their purpose in life. They know they have a unique contribution to make in this world, and they set out on a quest to find it. The key here is going through some trial and error along the way. You cannot find out what you're good at without simultaneously finding out what you're bad at. So don't be afraid of failure. Every failure can bring you one step closer to success – one step closer to discovering what you were made for.

Your Aunt Mimi will always think you can win the next season of American Idol, so find some people who will give honest feedback. Most of the time family and friends are too close to give you the unfiltered criticism you need. But here's the warning: if your journey of self-discovery stays self-focused for very long, it can turn into a cycle of selfishness. And selfish people rarely find their purpose.

When I was 19 and finishing up my first year of college, I didn't know what I wanted to do. At the time I dreamed of playing music full time, and I wasn't really sure if I should continue with college (that eventually changed, and I got my degree), but before I figured any of that out, I had to go through a season of discovery. I had to become an explorer.

Fortunately, I had a lot of friends who were exploring their own journeys, so we had lots to talk about. I took a semester off from school to explore life. The best job I could find was as – get this – a used car salesman. Not exactly glamorous. I had a thrift shop suit that I wore, and they even gave me business cards. What I learned was this: I can sell cars, but not without selling my soul. According to my boss, every car on our lot had been *"owned by a single old lady who drove the car to town and back a few times a week for groceries."* When anyone asked about a car's background, we were supposed to tell a version of this tall tale.

The trouble? I have a hard time lying to people, so I just couldn't do it. I worked there for about three months before quitting. Exploring your purpose can be hard, difficult work. I was embarrassed that I failed in the car business, but at least I still had my integrity.

Looking back, was the car gig a complete waste of time? No way. I learned about business, I learned about myself, I stood up for my beliefs, and most importantly, I failed forward – a concept I was reading about at the time in a book by John Maxwell.[28] In other words, by failing forward, I was letting that experience propel me further in my quest. The car gig showed me that life was much bigger than money. It taught me that I needed to be serving a bigger purpose – a purpose bigger than me, myself, and I.

FoLLoweRS

If you want to move beyond the explorer stage, you have to become a follower. Followers are people who find a bigger purpose worth pursuing, a cause worth joining, a dream worth living. They are workers who learn the joy of selfless giving and sacrifice. And as ironic as it may seem, becoming a good follower is one of the key factors in predicting your success as a leader.

A lot of people get stuck in a never-ending explorer stage because, even when they find a purpose, they still focus on themselves, so they fail to grow into leaders. They may even go as far as starting a business, declaring a vision, and hiring some staff. But no one wants to follow them. Why? Because selfish purposes reek like dog farts. I don't know any other way to say it. Everyone hates the smell except the dog itself, who remains completely unaware.

If your goals are no bigger than you, people will sniff you out. You can try to mask it with clever marketing and fancy search-engine-optimization, but you can't fool human beings on this one. It's in our blood to follow noble purposes, to dream bigger dreams, to live a greater story.

Your dog, on the other hand, will follow you anywhere. But why trust him? He can't even smell his own farts.

Leaders

Leaders embrace a greater purpose, one that focuses on making life better for other people. It's a purpose bigger than themselves. The best leaders are also the best followers. From a distance, you may not even see who or what they are following, but get closer and it becomes very clear. Great leaders are always searching for new ways to grow. They devour resources that will satisfy their love of learning and quench their thirst for wisdom. They pull inspiration from books, magazines, the internet, and strangers sitting next to them on airplanes. They listen to people who work underneath them and people of different social status. They seek advice from experts and mentors who have more life experience than them. In short, they are sponges of wisdom, sucking it up wherever they can find it.

A Leader is a giver – someone with a passionate purpose for serving people. They find their cause, and that drives them to want to develop other people around them, perhaps for the same cause, but often with no agenda at all other than the joy of contributing to someone else's growth in life.

We respect great leaders because we trust that they have everyone's best interests at heart. We follow them because they have a crystal clear purpose to serve a noble cause.

○ ○ ○

A clear purpose and a fight worth fighting for, this is how the journey from victim to leader begins.

You are uniquely shaped to be a leader in your area of life. Every experience you have, both positive and negative, can propel you forward or hold you back.

And it's 100% up to you. It's your choice to become…

VICTimPROOF.

CHAPTER 12 DISCUSSION GUIDE

1. Watch the Victimproof Video Curriculum DVD. Createspace.com/372336. Coupon Code: WGU4CUSK

2. Why do you think the Freedom Riders were motivated to stand up and step out as leaders?

3. Of the four types of people (Wanderers, Explorers, Followers, and Leaders), which do you think best describes where you are at personally? Why?

4. Why do you think so many teens get stuck in a never ending "explorer cycle?"

5. What are some of the unseen ways that the best leaders are also the best followers?

6. In the space below, write out one thing you will do to focus your mind and become VICTIMPROOF.

7. Write the name of one person and one resource (book, blog, etc.) you can follow to grow as a leader.

8. Take a look at the Victimproof Pledge on page 147. If you really want to become victimproof, read through it, print it, and sign it!

bonus chapter!

TOM'S SECRETS TO SUCCESS

If you skipped right to this section, shame on you. Go sit in the corner and give yourself a timeout. **There is no shortcut to success!** You can't microwave it, fast-forward it, or compact it. Success is achieved by sustained effort over time. With that said, teens always ask, "What are your secrets to success?" So I've compiled them into this brief chapter. If you want my full answers, please read the rest of the book!

SECRET 1 - BE A LEARNER

Developing the love of learning is the key to sustained growth as a person. I get so tired of talking to people who have learned all they ever want to know about life! It is the ultimate turn off – people who already know it all. So be teachable, and learn from your mistakes. Even better, find a mentor, and learn from the mistakes of others!

As a teen, this was the Burdick family for me. Today my mentor is a retired business man. When I asked him to be my mentor, he agreed, but only on one condition: that I be the one to determine when his advice was valuable and when it didn't apply to my situation. Now that is wisdom: being secure enough to know you don't have all the answers!

The biggest way I learn today is through "boring stuff" like books, blogs, PBS, and NPR. Pretty glamorous, I know. And then I go to bed early after playing shuffleboard with the neighbors. But for real, I consume valuable resources, I develop healthy relationships, and I tune out the static that clutters my mind. I love to learn, and I desire wisdom!

SECRET 2 - BE AN OWNER

I am the only person responsible for my life, my actions, my successes, and my failures. Outside forces and life circumstances come and go, so I resist the urge to blame anything on the actions of others or on situations that are out of my control.

I am not a victim.

I own my life. I own my results.

As an owner, I expect no one to do it for me. No one is going to give me permission, hand it to me on a silver platter, or give me the opportunity of my dreams. So I don't wait for opportunities – I create them. I weigh the risks, then I take action knowing that nothing of value comes without great sacrifice.

As an owner, I choose to step up to the plate of life knowing that every failure can bring me one step closer to success. I refuse to be a spectator, to wait around on-deck, or to stand in the batter's box waiting for the perfect pitch. I am not luckier than the rest, and I don't have the highest batting average, but simply because I take more swings, I create more success.

SECRET 3 - BE THE CHANGE

Gandhi said to be the change you want to see in the world. It's very easy to make commentary on why things should be better and why everyone else is doing it wrong, but it's another thing to help make it better.

Being the change means making the same decisions in private as you do in public. It means being a person of character and choosing the to do the right thing, even when it is inconvenient. It means realizing how the small decisions you make have a profound effect on yourself, your family, and your neighbors across the street and around the world.

The truth is that no one else can do it for you.

You have to step up and **be THe cHange!**

TAKE THE
VICTIMPROOF PLEDGE

I pledge to stand up to bullying –
to overcome social cruelty with kindness.

I commit to become victimproof –
to live free from bitterness and insecurity.

I choose to be bullyproof –
to set boundaries with abusive people.

I promise to become cultureproof –
to be an upstander and to be the change.

I take a stand.

I own my life.

I am... VICTIMPROOF

Signed_____ Signed_____
       (Tom Thelen)   (   )

ENDNOTES

[1] "The Map Has Been Replaced by the Compass."
Seth Godin's Blog. N.p., 21 Feb. 2012.
<http://sethgodin.typepad.com/.

[2] "Mahatma Gandhi Quotes - BrainyQuote." Famous
Quotes at BrainyQuote. N.p., n.d. Web. 21 Aug.
2012. <http://www.brainyquote.com/quotes/.

[3] "Matthew 18:21-22." Holy Bible: New International
Version. Grand Rapids, Mich.: Zondervan, 2005. Print.

[4] "Bullying Statistics 2010." BullyingStatistics.Org, n.d.
Web. 18 Feb. 2012. <http://www.bullyingstatistics.org/
content/bullying-statistics-2010.html>.

[5] "A Brief History of the Olweus Bullying Prevention
Program." Violence Prevention Works. Hazelden,
n.d. Web. 21 Nov. 2011.
<http://www.violencepreventionworks.org/
public/olweus_history.page

[6] "Student Reports of Bullying and Cyber-Bullying."
National Center for Education Statistics. U.S.
Department of Education, 1 May 2011. Web. 13
Apr. 2012. <nces.ed.gov/pubs2011/2011316.pdf>.

[7] "Bullying Definition." StopBullying.gov. U.S.
Department of Health & Human Services, n.d.
Web. 18 July 2012. <http://www.stopbullying.gov/
what-is-bullying/definition/index.html>.

[8] World Scripture - The Golden Rule." Unification.
N.p., n.d. Web. 2 Dec. 2010.
<http://www.unification.net/ws/theme015.htm>.

[9] Holy Bible: New International Version. Grand
Rapids, Mich.: Zondervan, 2005. Print.

[10] "BRAVE - Bullying Resources and Values
Education." Family Resources Facilitation Program.
N.p., n.d. Web. 18 Aug. 2012.
<http://www.frfp.ca/BRAVE/bullying_stats.htm>.

[11] Kindrick, Dr. Kristi. "Cyberbullying Triples Suicide
Risk in Teens." YouTube. IMNG Medical Media,
22 May 2013. Web. 16 June 2013.
<http://youtu.be/vtTagtvYQBc>.

[12] "The Solution to Social Cruelty." TruthLocker.
ParentingPride, Inc., n.d. Web. 8 Dec. 2012.
<TruthLocker.com>.

[13] "BRAVE - Bullying Resources and Values
Education." Family Resources Facilitation Program.
N.p., n.d. Web. 18 Aug. 2012.
<http://www.frfp.ca/BRAVE/bullying_stats.htm>.

[14] "Motivation Overview." University of Rhode
Island. N.p., n.d. Web. 12 May 2012.
<http://www.uri.edu/research/lrc/
scholl/webnotes/Motivation.htm>.

[15] Berridge, K. C. The Debate Over Dopamine's Role In Reward: The Case For Incentive Salience. Psychopharmacology. 2007; 191:391-431.

[16] "Wreck-It Ralph (2012) - IMDb." Internet Movie Database. N.p., n.d. Web. 18 Feb. 2013. <http://www.imdb.com/title/tt1772341/>.

[17] "Waiting for 'Superman' (2010)." Internet Movie Database. IMDb, n.d. Web. 9 Nov. 2012. <http://www.imdb.com/title/tt1566648/>.

[18] Einstein, Albert. "Albert Einstein - Wikiquote." Wikiquote. N.p., n.d. Web. 28 Feb. 2012. <http://en.wikiquote.org/wiki/Talk:Albert_Einstein>.

[19] Rovell, Darren. "Beachbody's P90X Making Serious Money" CNBC.com. N.p., 9 June 2010. Web. <http://www.cnbc.com/>.

[20] Allen, David. Getting Things Done: The Art of Stress-Free Productivity. New York: Viking, 2001.

[21] Grusenmeyer, David. "Mission, Vision, Values & Goals." Cornell University. Cornell University, n.d. Web. 16 May 1013. <ansci.cornell.edu/pdfs/pdmission.pdf>.

[22] Miller, Donald. Blue like jazz. Nashville, Tenn.: Thomas Nelson; 2006.

[23] Abudi, Gina. "The Five Stages of Project Team Development." The Project Management Hut. N.p., 8 May 2010. Web. <http://www.pmhut.com/the-five-stages-of-project-team-development>.

[24] Covey, Stephen. "Involvement Quote by Stephen Covey." GoodReads.Com. N.p., n.d. Web. 18 Oct. 2012. <http://www.goodreads.com/quotes/133327-without-involvement-there-is-no-commitment-mark-it-down-asterisk>.

[25] "Freedom Riders (2010) - IMDb." Internet Movie Database. IMDb, n.d. Web. 18 Mar. 2012. <http://www.imdb.com/title/tt1558952/>.

[26] "Emancipation Proclamation." Wikipedia. N.p., n.d. Web. 26 Apr. 2010. <http://en.wikipedia.org/wiki/Emancipation_Proclamation>.

[27] "The History of CORE." CORE-online.org. N.p., n.d. Web. 18 Jan. 2013. <http://www.core-online.org/History/history.htm>.

[28] Maxwell, John C. Failing forward: turning mistakes into stepping-stones for success. Nashville, TN: Thomas Nelson Publishers, 2000. Print.

about the author

Tom Thelen, author of Victimproof, is a youth motivational speaker whose message on bullying prevention has reached over 500 youth audiences since 2002. He speaks at youth conferences and school assemblies teaching students how to break free from the victim mindset and how to stand up to bullying. Tom has been featured on PBS, CBS, The National Association of Student Councils, YMCA Leadership Summits, and The National Honor Society. As a youth speaker, Tom gives students practical strategies to "BE THE CHANGE" on their campus. His high-energy school assembly programs provide an experience students never forget. Tom lives in Michigan with his wife Casie and their four children.

GET THE VICTIMPROOF DVD CURRICULUM!

Purchase the full Victimproof DVD Curriculum (with 30 video lessons!) for 50%-OFF the retail price by visiting Createspace.com/372336. Coupon Code: WGU4CUSK. For bulk order discount rates, email: Cameron@CharacterPrograms.Org.

FOLLOW TOM ON THE WEB

 Official Site: http://TomThelen.com

 Facebook.com/Tom.Thelen.Speaker

 Youtube.com/ThomasRThelen

 Twitter.com/TomThelenSpeaks

BOOK TOM TO SPEAK AT YOUR SCHOOL

Contact Cameron Versluis, Booking Assistant
(616) 987-0444 | Cameron@CharacterPrograms.Org

Made in the USA
Charleston, SC
16 June 2014